How to Write a Play

The tween and teen guide to mastering artful storytelling.

How to Write a Play

The tween and teen guide to mastering artful storytelling.

David Dubczak

Conjunction Media

For Laura, who has the displeasure of reading my first drafts.

For my students, who have the displeasure of hearing about my first drafts.

And to all those with imagination, who have the displeasure of needing something to do with it.

Contents

How is this different from school?

I could have called this book, "What your teachers don't teach you," but that would be mean.

Your teachers aren't holding anything back from you. They just have an unruly audience of kids and teenagers who probably have no interest in writing any real plays and just want to know how to pass the test. If you're holding this book, you're probably not one of those people.

This book isn't for them; it's for you. *You're* going to Broadway.

This book also isn't like a lot of playwriting books. I wrote a lot of plays while reading through those books before things "clicked." I won't repeat what most of those books say. Some of the least helpful experiences in my playwriting life have been actual classes on how to write plays.

This is a book of all the things that have "clicked" with me, and that I have gone on to use with my students. You won't find beat sheets, fill-in-the-blank plotting templates, or anything like that. Beat sheets may work for some people, but only if you understand *why* they work.

Finally, you can substitute *play* for any form of storytelling, including book, screenplay, graphic novel, video game plot, or anything else that tells a story.

How to use this book

First, we'll understand what makes a story *good*. Then, we'll take that and apply it to writing a play. Mixed in with all of that are exercises on how to think creatively, along with advice on how to have the right mindset to assemble a good story.

Do read this book from beginning to end, and do the exercises. No, I don't think my words are so holy that you need to read all of them. Each chapter and each exercise builds off the previous, so don't skip anything if you want to understand it all.

Once we understand what makes a story good, we build our theme. Then, we build characters around the theme. Finally, we build the plot.

Once we have a theme, characters, and plot, we write.

Then the hard work begins.

the first two things to learn

I have to be brutally honest with you. Promise me you won't put this book down after you read it. Only read on once you have promised. Yes, you can take time to cry, but then pick it back up and start reading.

Ready?

Here you go:

You are nobody.

Okay, I'm glad you're back. Truly. Truth is, you're not *nobody* in my eyes because chances are I don't know you. But in the eyes of all the producers out there, the ones who make the decisions about which plays to produce and which plays to even read... you are nobody.

You're not famous. You don't have a rich uncle. You don't know anybody with connections.

Those people can use their fame and money and connections to get crappy plays produced. *You* cannot. The only chance you have of getting your play produced is if it is so doggone diggity good that it sets the producer's fingers on fire and the only way to put them out is to greenlight the production of your script.

The script that does that will probably not be your first one. Becoming that good takes a long time.

Most people don't write plays. If you have written even one, you're in the elite 0.1% of people on Earth. Be proud of the work you have done and then commit to getting better on your next one.

(And if you do have a rich uncle, have him call me. I'd like to talk to him about producing a play.)

My first play I produced was the eighth one I wrote. My second play produced was the twelfth one I wrote. I have only four scripts for sale on my website right now, and only two of them have been produced. Theatre companies need to sell tickets, and hot plays and famous writers sell tickets.

The rewards are enormous, but the fight can be excruciating when you're a nobody. The only way to be *somebody* is to keep going.

Another warning: don't let that advice put too much pressure on you. Here's the single best, most important piece of writing advice I have ever been given:

> ## *The only thing the first draft needs to do is exist.*

Perfect is the enemy of good. Too many writers get a third of the way through their project, realize their pages belong in the toilet rather than on stage, and give up. Don't do that.

Only the *final* draft needs to be good. There are no rules on how many drafts it takes to get to the final draft. Take as many as you need.

Now, get started. Let's look at what makes a story good.

What makes a story good?

the "Campfire theory" of storytelling

The elements of good storytelling are hard wired into our brains.

Humans have been on Earth in our current form for about 100,000 years. However, the first traces of any written language are only about 5,000 years old. That means, for the first 95,000 years of human existence, the only way we had of learning anything was through telling stories. Our brains literally evolved to learn through stories.

Our brains like stories that have a lesson. Our brains like to see our own lives through the hero of the story. It gives us hope that, if the hero can overcome hard things, we can too.

Little kids learn by watching the adults in their lives. Big kids and adults learn through stories, and you see this on full display anytime you see a thirty-year-old wearing a Hogwarts uniform, or dressed as a Jedi or one of the Avengers. This is called "Living vicariously," when you imagine your own life through the lives of the story's characters.

So, take any story you know, and imagine it being told around a campfire. Imagine somebody telling "Harry Potter" or "Cars" or "Finding Nemo" around a campfire. Why? What's the point? What would they be trying to teach?

Most of these lessons are so, so simple. They're basic human lessons and experiences that everyone has to deal with. Love, friendship, leadership, strength, selflessness, neighborliness. Most might call this "Theme."

Change

I'll discuss "Theme" in a moment, but first, I find it useful to talk about change. In almost every good story, we learn the theme through a character changing.

In a good story, the main character changes, but they are *forced* to change. Something happens to them that forces them to change, something they neither wanted nor asked for.

- In Toy Story, Woody is forced to change when Buzz shows up in Andy's room.
- In Finding Nemo, Marlin is forced to change when Nemo is kidnapped.
- In Cars, Lightning McQueen is forced to change when he's stuck in Radiator Springs.
- In Aladdin, Aladdin is forced to change when he gets stuck in the cave with Genie.

- Harry Potter is forced to change when he learns he's a wizard, and an incredibly important wizard at that.

This event is called the *Inciting Event*. Your teacher may have taught this to you like my teachers taught it to me. But my teachers never helped me make the connection that the inciting event is the first domino to fall in a long line of events that causes the character to *change.*

Now, think back to that lesson you're teaching around the campfire. At the beginning of the story, the character is unaware of the lesson. They don't live by the rules of the lesson. Woody is not a good leader, Marlin is not brave, and Lightning McQueen is selfish.

Then the inciting event happens, and it begins a series of events that lead to the character's change. These events transform the character. At the beginning of the story, the character is oblivious to the theme - they live a life opposite of the theme. By the end of the story, they are the perfect embodiment of the theme. Woody is a good leader. Marlin is brave and allows Nemo more freedom. Lightning McQueen is selfless, and people like him because he's a good person.

The events of the story force them to go from being who they were to who they become.

The Campfire Theory

Pick any story with which you are familiar. What story did you pick?

What is the **<u>big life lesson</u>** or **<u>universal human truth</u>** this story is teaching?

What are the events in the story that cause the hero to change? Be as specific as possible.

theme

Now, we'll talk about theme with one very important warning: you may not realize the theme of your play until after you have written the first draft.

Every teacher tells you to have a theme. They are right. But, writing a play is a long process. As you write, your characters interact, form scenes, and have moments. As you write, the theme evolves and, by the end, you realize your play is *actually* about something completely different from what you wanted it to be about.

And that is fine... if you're okay with that. Write the play you want. Let it be what you want it to be.

I consider theme to be two parts: *Thematic Idea* and *Thematic Question*.

Thematic Idea is your broad topic that centers around a universal human emotion. Love, forgiveness, compassion, unity, happiness, togetherness, struggle, resistance, bravery, wisdom, redemption, family, loss, and more. These are the lessons ancient humans taught around the campfire.

- Toy Story: Friendship
- Finding Nemo: Bravery
- Cars: Selflessness

Thematic Question takes one of these ideas and turns it into a question.

- Toy Story: Can you be friends with someone different from you?
- Finding Nemo: Do you need to be brave to conquer danger?
- Cars: Is putting others first better than putting yourself first?

Your story is the journey of answering that thematic question. You, as the writer, are making an argument: Yes, you can be friends with someone different from you. No, you don't need to be brave to conquer danger. Yes, putting others first is better than putting yourself first. Your play is like an essay, putting your characters in situations to answer that question. This is called a *thesis*.

At the beginning of your story, your character is a shining example of the *opposite* of your theme - an anti-theme, or *anti-thesis*. Through the events of your story, they not only learn the theme, but they become the embodiment of the theme.

These universal human emotions could only be taught through storytelling for 95,000 years. That's why our brains are literally hard-wired to look for them in a story. When we find them, we usually like it, especially if we can see a bit of ourselves in it.

What doesn't make a story good?

Any student of any language arts class has probably seen something like this, called the "Story Mountain."

One thing you won't find in this book is a story mountain template. The story mountain is an important part of storytelling, but it is *not* what makes the story good. The story mountain is all about *structure*. Many stories follow the story mountain structure and are still not *good*. What will make your story good is a solid and artful execution of the theme, and watching the character change from being the antithesis of the theme to the embodiment of the theme.

Basically: Write a good story with a good theme and a character who is forced to change, and you will *end up* with a story mountain.

Theme Exercises

Tell your story around the campfire

Pick a story you already know (don't make one up yet). Imagine this story being told around a campfire. Why are they telling it? What is the universal human emotion they are trying to teach?

Imagine a group of adults telling this story to a group of kids. What universal human lessons are they trying to teach their kids through this story?

First, identify the *Thematic Idea*, and the *Thematic Question*. Then, in as much detail as possible, write out the events that happen that take your character from being the opposite of the theme to the embodiment of the theme.

Thirty Tertiary Connections

Primary means "first." Secondary means "second." Here's a new word: *Tertiary*, which means "third."

Pick a universal human emotion, preferably something you want to write about. Write it in the center of a piece of paper and spend a minute thinking of all the words you can think of relating to that word. Those words are called *primary connections*.

Then, look at your primary connections, and spend some time thinking of 3-5 words relating to each of your primary connections. Those are called *secondary connections*.

Then, spend time thinking of 3-5 words that connect to each of your secondary connections. Those are called *tertiary connections*.

Spend enough time doing this that you have not 30 words total, but 30+ *tertiary connections*.

Keep this. This is the fuel that will feed your story as you write.

Creativity Tip

Word webs are one of the most useful creative tools in your toolbox! Creativity depends on finding connections and building upon them.

Creative Thinking is also a muscle that can be strengthened with exercise. So, don't fret if it's hard at first! Always shoot for 30+ tertiary connections, because that's where you'll find your creative ideas.

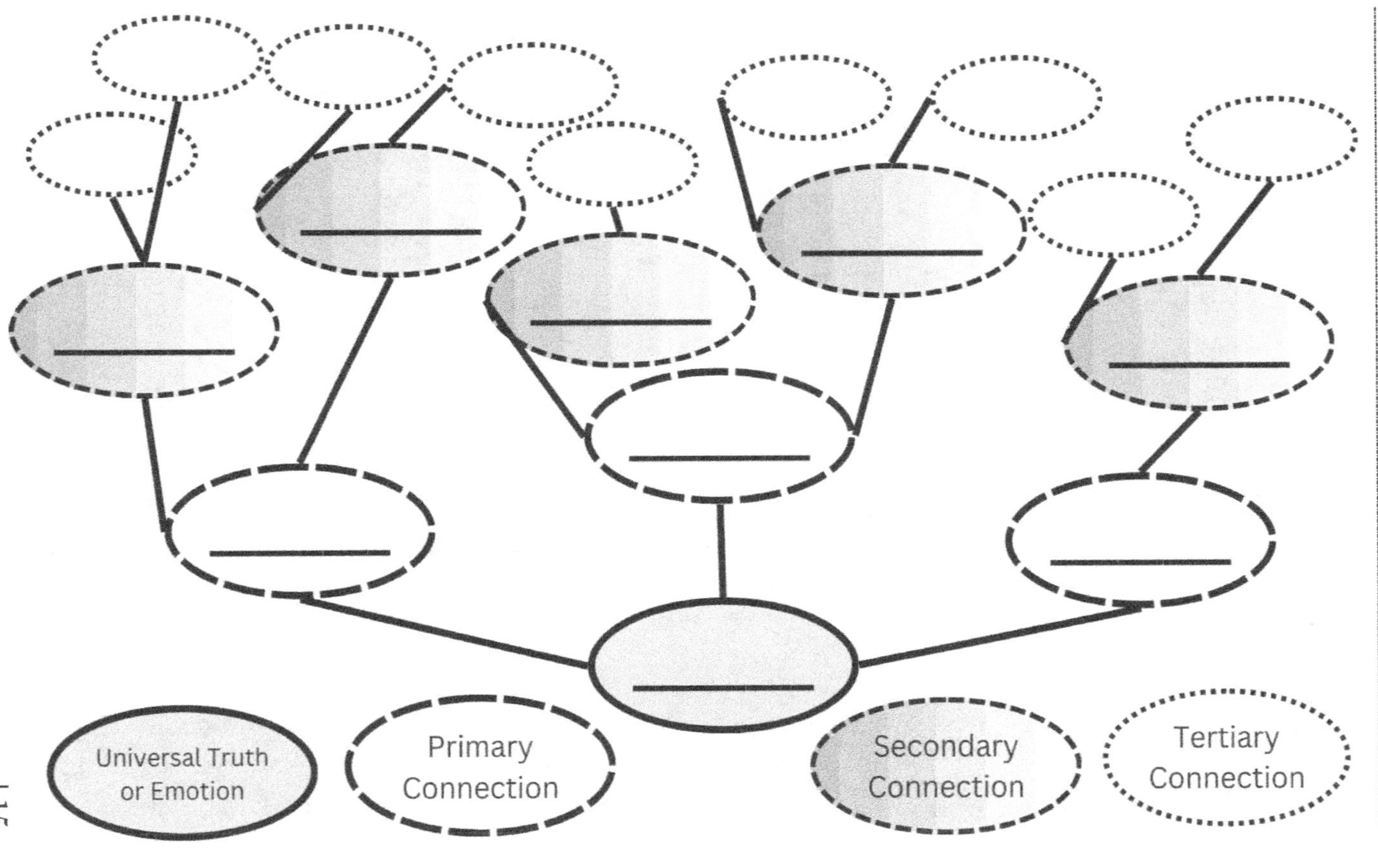

Universal Truth or Emotion
Primary Connection
Secondary Connection
Tertiary Connection

Characters

Plays are tricky things. Some plays only have two characters, while others have thirty or more. Sometimes, you write whatever your imagination drives you to write. Sometimes, you have limits imposed by others, such as a theatre company telling you that they only have eight actors to work with.

In the case of <u>Guttenberg, the Musical</u>, the show has around 20 characters performed by only two actors switching out hats as they jump back and forth between characters. Often, actors can be doubled or tripled, where supporting actors may play two or three different characters.

(I once acted in a play where I played a crippled old man whose fingers were turning black from radiation necrosis. I stored makeup remover wipes in the pocket of my bathrobe, which also covered a triple-breasted suit. When a scene ended, I flew backstage while wiping the black makeup from my fingertips, threw off the bathrobe, donned a pair of glasses, and emerged onstage 30 seconds later as a young and healthy posh corporate lawyer determined to delay the lawsuits long enough that the plaintiffs would die before their court date).

First, let's start by building your main character, the protagonist, the one who needs to change.

Some writers write elaborate, pages-long backstories on their characters before they begin. I've never found that helpful. While you don't need to have planned out every moment of your character's life before you begin writing, a few things are helpful to know and can guide you while you write. For this, we can make a *Character Tree*.

Character tree

I know, this looks more like a stick figure than a tree. It is. It also sounds better than "Character Stick Figure." Call it whatever you like - it's your character tree. If you call it something else while I'm not around you, you won't hurt me. If you call it something else while I *am* around you, the most you'll do is confuse me.

First, start with the **Heart**. The heart represents the character's desires - what they truly, truly want deep inside. Imagine your character as the center of a musical. Often, in a musical, the main character sings an "I Want..." song.

- Arial (The Little Mermaid): "I want to be where the people are..."
- Simba (The Lion King): "I just can't wait to be king!"
- Leo Bloom (The Producers): "I wanna be a producer... 'cause it's everything I'm not."
- Alexander Hamilton (Hamilton): "I wanna be in the room where it happens."

- Quasimodo (Hunchback of Notre Dame): "If I could spend one day out there."

Here's the key: Their heart is who they *want* to be... they are not that thing yet! Their desire to be that thing, be that way, have that item, reach that goal... that desire is what will drive their story.

Second, think of the **Brain**. The brain represents the character's skills, what they're good at. Whatever you write at this stage, you don't need to stick with forever, but whatever they do in their current life, they are good at something.

- Both Anakin and Luke Skywalker (Star Wars) are elite pilots.
- Lightning McQueen (Cars) is a championship-caliber racecar driver.
- Woody (Toy Story) is a good group organizer.

But now, we move on to the **Stomach**. The stomach represents the character's fears, what they're afraid of. We see this very clearly in both Star Wars and Harry Potter. In Star Wars Episode V, <u>The Empire Strikes Back</u>, Luke Skywalker enters a cave strong in the dark side. Inside, he's confronted by a vision of Darth Vader. During a brief lightsaber battle, he cuts off Darth Vader's head. After rolling to a stop on the ground, the faceplate blows off the mask, revealing underneath Luke's own face.

Yes, Luke is afraid that, within him, lay all the same ingredients as Darth Vader and, if he's not careful, Luke's own destiny is the same. He's on a very slippery slope to becoming Darth Vader.

In Harry Potter, both Harry and Voldemort can speak to snakes. Throughout the series, Harry is on the same slippery slope - a part of Voldemort literally lives within Harry. Harry can easily become just as evil as Voldemort.

Your character may be afraid of being a loser, or becoming evil, or being alone. They may be afraid of spiders or snakes. Perhaps they're afraid of failure or, even more interesting, afraid of success.

To do this well: Think back to your theme. Both your dreams and fears should be related to the theme. If your character dreams of a quiet life on the reef with his son (Marlin in Finding Nemo), a fear of failure and a fear of loss would tie into the theme of bravery and letting your kid grow up.

Both the character's dreams and fears drive them and cause them to take action. Those are the legs.

The **Right Leg** are the character's heart actions. These are the things the character might be willing to do to move toward their goals, dreams, and desires. That's rather easy to come up with.

What's harder is the **Left Leg**, or actions the character takes because of their fears. The actions someone takes are not always to avoid their fears. It makes sense for a character who is afraid of snakes to avoid snakes. Sometimes, however, they create anti-snake defenses around their home, or they take out their fears on the snakes themselves by hunting for and killing them and impaling their heads on stakes and displaying them around their fortress as a warning to other snakes.

Further, a character who is afraid of looking dumb might work extra hard to be sure they're always right; a character who is afraid of being alone might make friends with bad people just because they're willing to be friends.

A character who fears physical challenges because they're out of shape may avoid physical challenges, or take on physical challenges in order to get stronger. Either way, these are intentional actions.

Left Leg actions are taken to avoid their fears, confront their fears, or fill the empty buckets that scare them. Bottom line is these are all *actions*.

Character Tree

Character Creating

Imagine a character. First, fill in the blanks:
______[name]______ the ____[trait]____ who
______[problem]______. Play around with several variations until you have something interesting and seems worthy of being your protagonist. For example:

- Marlin the clownfish whose son was kidnapped.
- Woody the favorite toy who is suddenly replaced.
- Curley the thief who wants to win a million dollars.
- Miles the blind who lost his dog.
- Quinn the one-legged who failed math class.
- Captain McSquiggles the cat who wants to be a dog.

Once you have an interesting character, take a blank sheet of paper and fill out a character tree. Make up details that are interesting and help give you a direction to go when you start writing.

At this point, however, don't become too attached to any of your ideas. Anything can change until you have a final draft. If your story starts going in a different direction and you want to change the fears, or the right leg/left leg actions, don't be afraid to do this.

In the words of Captain Barbosa from Pirates of the Caribbean, "They're more of what you'd call *guidelines* rather than actual *rules*."

Pro Tip: After you write your first draft, go back and fill out a more detailed character tree using everything you now know about this character. Is this what you wanted when you started? Do your character's actions now align with their goals and fears? Should you go back and change anything in the draft to keep your character's actions making sense throughout the play?

Villains

Not every story has a villain. Some stories are artfully crafted villain-less. In *The Martian*, Mars itself is the villain. In *Apollo 13*, space is the villain. In Ken Ludwig's *Moon Over Buffalo*, the protagonist is his own worst enemy with his own buffoonish antics. This is a tactic common in comedy, in which the protagonist fights their own inner demons rather than any one particular foe.

My favorite examples of this are in the classic TV sitcom *Frasier*, a show widely regarded as being the "master of the farce," a type of heightened situational comedy. For shining examples, see episodes such as *Ham Radio, Merry Christmas Mrs. Moskowitz, A Lilith Thanksgiving,* and *Motor Skills.*

Character Creator

To do this well, write your entire name list before writing any traits. Then, write your entire trait list before writing any problems. After writing your entire problem list, mix and match and have fun!

_________________ the _______________ who_______________.
(name)   (trait)   (problem)

Mack   the   penguin   who   farted
Dr. Herman the   Sheriff   who   got lost
Shirley   the   clumsy   who won the lottery
Capt. Wiggles the   short   who needs a friend

_________________ the _______________ who_______________.

_________________ the _______________ who_______________.

_________________ the _______________ who_______________.

_________________ the _______________ who_______________.

_________________ the _______________ who_______________.

_________________ the _______________ who_______________.

_________________ the _______________ who_______________.

_________________ the _______________ who_______________.

_________________ the _______________ who_______________.

_________________ the _______________ who_______________.

(We'll discuss comedy more in-depth in a later chapter).

Even in the Pixar films Cars and Finding Nemo, we see no obvious villain. Lightning McQueen's worst enemy is himself, and Marlin's big battle is against the ocean.

However, everyone loves a good, well-crafted villain. Darth Vader, Voldemort, Jafar, Scar, the evil sorceress or the cunning thief - the villains give your protagonist a tough fight.

Here's the biggest lightbulb moment I have ever had about the villain:

> ## *The villain represents the opposite of the hero.*

The villain represents everything the hero stands against but, more interestingly, the villain is who the hero is afraid of becoming. In my own play, <u>Not a Murder Mystery</u>, our hero, Curley, is a con-artist swindler who has all the same ingredients as the villain, the con-artist Professor Mayberry. It would be very easy for Curley to be just like him. The story, then, is the story of how Curley *does not* become the Professor.

In my own book <u>Jasper Berry and the Order of the Time Watchers</u>: [SPOILER ALERT], the twist at the end reveals that our protagonist Jasper quite literally grows up to be the villain Hayalet.

Star Wars is the story of how Luke Skywalker does not become Darth Vader, and Harry Potter is the story of how Harry does not become Voldemort. As the ball of the story rolls down hill, hit a rock just the wrong way or a nudge in just the wrong direction, and they very much could.

How to develop a good villain

Think back to your *Thematic Question*. Ideally, it is something with both a "yes" and "no" answer. For example, "Can you be friends with someone different from you?" The lesson of your story leads you to the answer, "yes." The events of the story force your character to change in the direction of that "yes."

But what if the answer is "no?" Why *can't* you be friends with someone different from you? *This* is the viewpoint of your villain. These two sides of the argument are where the words *protagonist* (pro...) and *antagonist* (anti...) come from.

To develop your villain, think through some reasons why the answer to your thematic question would be "no." Be very convincing. Imagine you're in a life-and-death debate and your life depends on convincing people the answer is "no." Imagine your life depends on convincing people that you *can't* be friends with someone different from you, that putting others first *isn't* better than putting yourself first.

For the purpose of this exercise, you must believe your villain. Your audience should listen to them and think, "Well, maybe they have a point?"

In my own play <u>The Healer</u>, Dr. Christoph Brenner was sent to medical school by his Amish-like community in the early 1900s. When he returns, his style of practicing medicine and treating patients goes against many of the community's traditional practices. The story's villain, Frau Frieda, says this to him after she prevents Dr. Brenner from treating a deathly ill young woman because it is improper for a young unmarried man to spend time with a married woman without her husband present:

FRIEDA. I didn't write these rules. They are ancient, sacred, and holy. Following these rules is the way we learn to live as a community.

CHRISTOPH. But surely we can make an exception when a life is at stake!

FRIEDA. *(Beat. She exhales, pondering).* If we cross this line, where does it stop? This line exists because it helps us build strong families. We know where this line is, but if we cross it, where do we draw a new one? God gave us this line; who are we to say He is wrong and ours is better? *(beat)* There will be consequences if you cross that line, Christoph.

Every villain thinks they're the hero. Darth Vader thinks he's bringing peace and security to the Empire; Voldemort believes letting mudbloods practice magic makes all magic weaker; Jafar (Aladdin) believes the Sultan is dumb and weak and that he can do better.

When you write the villain, *they* believe they're right. Give them a convincing argument.

Villain Exercise

Write a page answering your thematic question from the perspective of your villain. The villain would answer the opposite of the hero. Be convincing. The villain fully believes every word that they say, that the answer to your thematic question is, "no!"

Remember, you have a *thesis* that answers your dramatic question. The villain's point of view is the antithesis - the *anti-thesis*, or opposite point of view. Though you are making the argument that they're wrong, their argument should be compelling enough that we at least wonder if they might have a point.

Other Characters

Characters and your hero's goal

The purpose of other characters is to move your protagonist either toward their goal or away from it. Every scene should end with your hero being either closer to their goal or further from it (something we'll discuss in the plot chapter). Very rarely are characters just *there*.

If a character doesn't exist to move your hero, they represent and demonstrate the world in which the hero lives.

In <u>Finding Nemo</u>, every character Marlin meets on the way to finding Nemo moves him in some way. First, Dori wanders haplessly into the dangers that Marlin might otherwise avoid. The anglerfish, the sharks, the school of fish, the turtles, and the jellyfish all serve to move Marlin either closer to or further away from his goal.

Supporting Character Exercise

Go back to your mind map about theme. Use this to help you determine characters that can help your hero move either toward or away from their goal.

For example, if your theme is *love*, you may have made connecting words of *togetherness, friendship, support,* and *joy*. These can all represent characters that can help move your hero toward your goal. You may also have made connections of *fear, mistrust,* and *jealousy*. Each of these can be turned into characters that would move your hero backwards, such as a jealous moment upsetting a potential love interest.

Characters and your audience

People of all ages and all walks of life may watch your play. Kids, rich old retired men, career-minded go-getters, and mothers struggling with their unruly kids.

Remember the campfire theory: people will learn and appreciate the lessons of the story when they can see a bit of themselves in it. Having a wide variety of different types of characters helps give more members of your audience someone to whom they can relate.

Characters and theatre companies

As much as we playwrights want to let our imaginations go wild, theatre companies often have limits on the number and type of characters a play can have.

Smaller theatres may have fewer members, or a smaller pool of actors. In which case, they may not be able to perform plays with more than 5-10 actors.

You may need to write parts that can be doubled or tripled, in which one actor plays two or three different characters. If you do this, you obviously can't have those characters on the stage at the same time.

If you're writing for schools, schools often have far more female actresses participate in their shows than male actors. Plays with more parts for actresses tend to sell better. A play that needs too many males is unlikely to get picked up. Consider having more female parts, or more gender-flexible parts for which the gender of the actor isn't important.

Plot

As an inexperienced writer, I came across a "beat sheet," where another kind writer tried to guide us newbies by saying, "Do this here, this here, and this here, and you'll have a blockbuster."

Don't follow a beat sheet. They don't work. Following a beat sheet will usually mean you randomly generate plot points to fit beats that don't connect back to anything else. Your theme gets lost, and your lessons around the campfire get confused. Don't follow beat sheets.

I won't give you a beat sheet or a story mountain. Instead, I'll give you a few key sections of a particular type of story called the <u>Hero's Journey</u>, and explain the *why* behind these sections. You need to understand *why* you're writing a scene, not just what sort of scene should be happening here.

Some people confuse studying the Hero's Journey and think it's one type of story among many. No. The Hero's Journey is an illustration of the events of a story that cause your character to change. *Every good story will change your hero.*

Don't try to follow the "beats" of the Hero's Journey. Think about how and why your hero needs to change, and what might be the most interesting and compelling ways to show this.

Also, there's a difference between *plot* and *scenes*. All your scenes together represent your plot. *Scenes* are a different chapter.

How to plot really well

When you're trying to figure out, "What do I do now?" Don't do the first thing that comes to mind. Don't do the second thing that comes to mind. Go with the third or the fourth or the fifth.

Swirling in your brain right now are all the plays and movies you've ever seen and all the books you've ever read. The first thing that comes to mind will probably be something from those, something everyone's seen before.

Audiences love it when you set them up to expect something, and then delight them by giving them something unexpected that's even better.

Before you decide what happens next, write down five or more ideas. The ones that were the hardest to come up with just might be your best.

Why study the Hero's journey?

Joseph Campbell was an anthropologist who wanted to study differences in storytelling across cultures, both modern and ancient cultures from around the world.

Campbell made an interesting discovery: the basic principles of storytelling seemed to be shared between all these different cultures all across the world and all across time. He published his findings in a book called <u>The Hero with a Thousand Faces</u>.

Did I rip off Joseph Campbell when I shared with you the campfire theory? *Maaaayyyyybbbeeee....*

No, I summarized a big, long, confusing book into its most important principle: stories were used for most of human history to teach our most important lessons, and for that reason the elements of good storytelling are built into our brains.

Joseph Campbell found the same basic hero recurring in story after story after story around the world, from modern day America to ancient Babylonia. The point in understanding this is not to copy the Hero's Journey template, but to understand *why* this hero keeps coming back up: we see something of ourselves in this hero's journey, something that's important for us to learn. If the hero can change, if the hero can defeat their inner demons or their external foes, so can we. That's why we like it.

So now, let's start your story at the beginning.

the Hero's World

Every hero has a life they live before *The Thing* happens. *The Thing* may be bad, like a car accident or a meteor strike or getting bit by a radioactive spider. *The*

Thing may be good, like getting a promotion or winning the lottery or meeting the romantic partner of their dreams.

Whatever *The Thing* is, your hero had a life before *The Thing* happened. The two most interesting places to start a story are in the middle of their life right before *The Thing* happens, or in the few moments right after *The Thing* happens.

Every story is the story of your hero changing, but we don't know why they need to change unless we see what their life was like before *The Thing*. We need to see why Woody needs to be a better friend or why Lightning McQueen needs to be less self-absorbed. We need to see what's going on in your character's life that makes the change necessary.

Then *The Thing* happens. It happens *to* your hero. It changes your hero and they can't avoid it.

But it doesn't mean they can't try. Their quiet life, their nice life, *the life they know* is interrupted by *The Thing*. It may not have even been the greatest life, but the devil they know beats the devil they don't. Change is scary and they don't want to change.

But, *The Thing* has happened. Whether they like it or not, their life is forever changed. Your character now has a problem they need to solve. This problem is **important** enough that they *must* solve it. They cannot sit back and ignore it. Ignoring it would be to ignore who they are at their core.

When Buzz Lightyear usurped Woody's position as Andy's "favorite toy," Woody couldn't just ignore it.

When Nemo was kidnapped, Marlin couldn't just ignore it.

When Darth Vader killed Luke's aunt and uncle, Luke couldn't just ignore it.

When Lightning McQueen was arrested for tearing up the road in Radiator Springs, he couldn't just ignore it.

After *The Thing* happens, their life is no longer the same. This doesn't mean, however, they have to accept this *yet*. In fact, many people will try to solve The Thing *so that* they can go back to their previous life!

- Woody wanted to get rid of Buzz so that he could go back to being Andy's favorite.
- Marlin wanted rescue Nemo so he could go back to his same old life on the reef.
- Lightning McQueen just wanted to get out of Radiator Springs and return to the racetrack.

It's not a rule that this *always* needs to happen. I'm not sure Luke Skywalker wanted to return to being a moisture farmer after avenging his aunt and uncle's death. However, Luke did resist the call to become a Jedi until he realized - through his aunt and uncle's death - that returning to the simple moisture farming life was impossible.

Harry Potter certainly didn't want to return to the Dursley's. However, from the moment Hagrid first picked him up, returning to a life unaware of wizardry is impossible.

In your hero's home world, we see why their change is necessary. We see why Luke Skywalker and Harry Potter need to learn how to take on a world and a galaxy bigger than themselves.

the trials

In the second act of the story, the hero tries to solve their problem, but they are *not yet ready*. They are not yet *good enough*. This, however, does not stop them from trying.

Throughout this part of the story, they actively try to solve their problem and reach their goal. But, because they're not yet ready, they fail. They make mistakes. They may not yet even realize they're not ready.

They can't really solve their problem until they've learned their lessons and, at this point, they have not yet learned their lessons! It is here, in the trials, where they learn their lessons.

Think back to your dramatic question. What are the arguments *against* your thesis? Here, your hero can experience the full weight of these arguments.

Marlin (Finding Nemo) believes the ocean is a big and scary place full of danger, and that's why he needs to protect Nemo. Now, in the big open ocean, he experiences all of that danger first hand! He gets attacked by anglerfish, sharks, and explosive mines!

Sometimes, trying to solve their problem makes their problem even worse, such as when Woody pushes Buzz out the window and they *both* wind up lost. It's important to allow your hero to make mistakes.

Nonetheless, your hero is not yet good enough to solve their problem. In <u>Star Wars: The Empire Strikes Back</u>, Luke Skywalker hastily moves to confront Darth Vader. Vader *dominates* an epic lightsaber battle that ends with him cutting off Luke's hand. In <u>Harry Potter and the Order of the Phoenix</u>, Harry and his friends rush to try to save Sirius Black, who they believe to be in peril in the Department of Mysteries. They, however, do not yet have enough command over magic to defeat Voldemort's Death Eaters who laid this challenge as a trap. They only narrowly escape when the Order of the Phoenix comes to their rescue, a rescue that results in Sirius Black's death.

To write the trials, think again of your thematic idea and thematic argument. Brainstorm several answers to these two questions:

- What makes life difficult if you don't understand the theme?
- What would be the hardest ways to go about learning this lesson?

What makes it hard to learn the lesson?

- When it requires abandoning your old way of life.
- When it requires making decisions you don't want to make.
- When it requires accepting a truth that you don't want to admit.

All of these require... you guessed it: *change*.

It's easy to consider something like the Hero's Journey and imagine the trials to be big, dramatic moments of epic fight scenes and overpowering foes. However, not every story is an action/adventure story.

The 1999 film <u>October Sky</u> follows the true story of Homer Hickam, a high school boy who grew up in Coalwood, West Virginia - a coal mining town, as the name suggests. In Coalwood, every single person in town was a coal company employee who either worked in the mine or in a job that supported the miners. As Hickam himself put it, even the town preacher was a coal company employee. The only job of the high school was to prepare boys to be coal miners and girls to be coal miners' wives.

The Event in Homer's life is seeing the Soviet satellite Sputnik fly overhead and deciding that he wanted to grow up to be not a miner, but a rocket scientist. He and his friends go about learning to build their own rockets.

It's not a movie filled with lightsaber battles, sorcery, and martial arts. In Homer Hickam's story, the trials include a father who doesn't support his ambitions, the struggle to obtain the right materials, not understanding the science behind why their rockets keep blowing up, a forest fire blamed on the boys' experiments, and Homer needing to put his rockets aside and work in the mine after his father's injury.

Even lighthearted comedies and, dare I say it, love stories have trials. The trials can be losing a job, the judgment of others who don't know all the facts, or losing your car keys. Here are some examples of the trials from lighthearted comedies:

Elf (2003): Buddy, a human raised by elves, goes to New York City to find his biological father. He tries to fit in and bring Christmas cheer but fails hilariously. From drinking syrup-laden coffee to causing chaos at his father's office, his trials are a series of misguided attempts to blend in with a world he doesn't yet understand. His mistakes add complications and teach him about family, acceptance, and boundaries.

School of Rock (2003): Dewey Finn, a down-and-out musician, poses as a substitute teacher to make money, intending to turn his class into a band for a contest. In his trials" he faces challenges from parents, the principal, and the students' initial lack of skill. Every step seems to create more problems, especially when he encourages rebellious behavior in kids who aren't ready for it. Ultimately, these trials help Dewey realize he must respect the students' talents and work with them collaboratively.

The Princess Diaries (2001): Mia Thermopolis is thrust into the role of princess and has to go through a series of "royal" trials, like learning etiquette, giving speeches, and handling public scrutiny. Her awkward, humorous mistakes—like accidentally setting a man's sleeve on fire or slipping on the palace floor—reinforce that she's not yet ready for the crown. These failures help Mia discover her own values and strength beyond royal expectations.

Push and Pull Factors — "The Perfect Ballgame."

Not every trial your hero experiences needs to be bad. They don't need to lose every trial. In fact, winning a few gives them (and us) hope.

Your character has a goal. Some events move your character *toward* the goal, while others move them *away*. I like to call these "Push and Pull Factors."

Famed American playwright David Mamet wrote an essay titled <u>The Perfect Ballgame</u>. You should Google this and read it in his own words. But, the gist of the "perfect ballgame" is this:

What's more interesting to watch? A ballgame where one team comes out and pummels the other team into submission from the very first play? Or, a game with backs and forths, where Our Team is the underdog and they start with a strong play, but then face a series of setbacks against a stronger opponent. They end the first half down, but with a glimmer of hope. In the second half, right as things are looking up, we face a threat: an error, mistake, or a bad call by the refs. As Our Team recovers, we lose our best player due to injury and have to call the unproven third-string player off the bench, who unexpectedly leads us to just barely squeaking by with an underdog win!

(Though he wrote this in 1998, <u>The Perfect Ballgame</u> seemingly predicted, beat-by-beat, the Chicago Cubs' World Series game seven victory in 2016).

Your hero needs to lose in order to learn, but they need to win to give hope. Writing a riveting back-and-forth keeps your audience on the edge of their seats.

How to do this really well

Remember: audiences love it when you set them up to expect something, and then delight them by giving them something unexpected that's even better.

When you need to decide what happens next, sit down and make a list of everything your audience might expect to happen next. Then, don't do any of those things. Delightfully surprise them with something better.

But, don't put your hero through random trials just because the story mountain says to put the trials here. Connect their trials back to your theme. Understand and know your character: What are they afraid of? What are their weaknesses? Hit them with exactly those things during the trials.

the Confrontation

At some point, your hero is ready. They have spent the entire story learning through failure. They have spent the entire story becoming stronger and more knowledgeable about the world into which you have thrust them.

Now, your hero is ready to reach their goal. However, we have a twist: their goal is no longer their goal.

The trials have changed them. They're not just stronger, but smarter and wiser. They realize what they originally wanted isn't actually what they wanted in the first place. They want something different, something better.

- Luke Skywalker wanted to be a Jedi to kill Darth Vader and avenge his father's death. After the trials, he confronts Vader not to kill him, but to save his father.
- Marlin (Finding Nemo) wants to save Nemo and bring him back to their safe life on the reef. After the trials, he realizes he wants Nemo to *thrive*, which may mean not hovering over him and protecting him from everything, but allowing Nemo to face challenges for himself.
- Lightning McQueen (Cars) wants to win the Piston Cup. After the trials, he realizes being a good person and competing with good sportsmanship is more important than winning at all costs.
- Homer Hickam (October Sky) wants to be a rocket scientist. After the trials, he realizes what's really driving him is a desire to show Coalwood that the bright young people of Coalwood have more options for their future than just mining coal.

Rejecting the Old Goal

But one challenge still remains: despite everything they have learned, the call of their home world calls one more time. They have one more opportunity to get what they thought they wanted at the beginning of the story.

- Luke Skywalker, with Darth Vader wounded and defenseless on the ground, has one more opportunity to kill him.
- Lightning McQueen has a runaway lead for the Piston Cup when The King crashes.
- Marlin has reached the dentist's office to rescue Nemo right as Nemo is about to attempt his own dangerous flight to freedom.

This is where we show that the hero has *learned* and *changed*. They reject their old goal in order to achieve their new goal.

- Luke Skywalker throws away his lightsaber and announces to the Emperor, "You've failed, your highness. I am a Jedi, like my father before me."
- Lightning McQueen slams on the brakes and comes to a stop just feet before the finish line, and reverses to come to The King's aid. He loses the Piston Cup to give The King a dignified finish.
- Marlin realizes that he can't really get what he wants unless he trusts that Nemo can take care of himself. Instead of rescuing Nemo, he trusts Nemo's plan and allows Nemo to rescue himself.

This sometimes comes at a cost. Rejecting their old ways subjected Luke Skywalker to a Force-lightning attack from the Emperor; Lightning McQueen lost the Piston Cup; Marlin thought Nemo died.

How to do the confrontation really well

Your hero can make a choice between their old goal (the easy way) and their new goal (the hard way). They can only achieve their new goal by rejecting their old goal.

And, once again, don't give your audience what they expect. In the words of the producers of the iconic sitcom Friends: Give your audience what they want, but not in the way they're expecting to get it.

the Resolution

Having won, your character now returns to their life, but it's a new life, not the one they thought they wanted.

Woody and Buzz return to Andy's room not as competitors for Andy's love, but hoping that Andy finds joy in all his toys.

Lightning McQueen rejoins the Piston Cup circuit with new friends and a coveted sponsorship he earned by helping The King.

Marlin and Nemo return to the reef to a much more fulfilling life, one where Marlin isn't constantly hovering over and protecting Nemo, and Nemo experiences the joys of the freedom appropriate for someone his age.

Harry Potter defeated Voldemort and helps rebuild Hogwarts not just as "the one who killed Voldemort," but as one who explicitly rejected ever having the kind of power Voldemort had by destroying the Elder Wand to which he was justly entitled.

Homer Hickam returns to Coalwood after winning the National Science Fair. Though winning the fair gave him his ticket away from what he used to think was a dead-end town, he returns with an appreciation for the people of Coalwood, the help they gave him, and the hope they see in him.

How to do the resolution really well

At the beginning of your story, when you were first showing the hero and their world, your hero exemplified the *opposite* of your thematic question. Now, they are the *embodiment* of the thematic question.

In the end, your hero didn't get what they thought they wanted; they got something better.

When I don't know what should come next?

Two key questions:

What's the worst that can happen right now?

What is my hero the least prepared to handle?

Those are two great things to make come next!

Likewise, ask, "What is my hero good at? Comfortable with?" Then, throw the exact opposite at them and see how they handle it.

Plot: Comedy vs. Drama

Don't make the mistake of thinking the Hero's Journey is reserved for dramas and adventure stories. Not at all! The biggest difference between a drama and a comedy is how the hero goes about trying to solve their problem.

In a comedy, your hero has a key character flaw. A character flaw is something undesirable about a character: They're a liar, they're arrogant and think they're the best, they're indecisive and can't make a decision, they can't admit mistakes, or anything else you can think of that are not good qualities of a person.

In a comedy, your hero is willing to do anything and everything to solve the problem *except* resolve their key character flaw. It's funny when we, as the audience, know what they should do and the hero is willing to do anything except that!

However, your character's actions shouldn't be random or nonsensical. Your character is actually trying to solve the problem! They lack the skills, knowledge, or ability to solve the problem, but that doesn't stop them from trying.

Their lack of skill or ability may make the problem worse as they continually make the wrong choices, and these choices often cause problems for other people.

Before you write, take your character's central flaw and make a list of 5-10 things this character definitely *would not do*. For example, an arrogant character definitely would not:

- Ask for help
- Admit failure
- Admit someone else is better
- Believe their struggles are caused by something *they* did
- Believe they made a mistake

What will make your story funny is putting your character in situations that are so easily solved by doing one of those things. We as the audience will know your character just needs to ask for help! But, as an arrogant person, that is the one thing they will not do!

In my own <u>Not a Murder Mystery</u>, our hero is a thief and con-artist named Curley, who is a stowaway aboard the ship *The Mississippi Belle* where her brother works as a steward. Curley swears she's leaving crime behind her and just needs to get up north, where she's taking over her mom's store.

However, when there's a murder aboard and a passenger offers a million dollar reward for winning the prize, Curley can't help herself. She dons a disguise and creates the identity of mister "Abel Underwood," a flamboyant southern gentleman. Curley hatches a scheme to win the prize by framing

"Mr. Underwood" for the murder, so Curley can turn him in and win the prize for herself.

Curley's goal is to be able to leave crime behind her. If she keeps her head down, continues to work as a steward with her brother's help, and tries to avoid controversy, she'll win by being able to make it to her mother's store. *But she simply cannot help it.* She's a con artist and, thus, the best way to solve her problem is with a con.

In Jim Carrey's <u>Bruce Almighty</u>, Bruce complains to God that he could make the world better if only he had God's power. So, God comes down and makes Bruce God for a week!

But God has responsibilities. He needs to listen to and answer prayers. Bruce, however, just wants to use God's power for personal gain, so he tries to avoid answering prayers by setting up prayer emails, prayer post-its, and prayer file cabinets.

Frustrated that the more prayers he answers, the more prayers come in, he uses his prayer email to select "Yes to all." Chaos ensues when everyone's prayers are answered no matter how nonsensical, leading to a quip from one woman, "I've lost seventeen pounds on the Krispy Kreme diet!"

As you work through your plot, ask yourself at any given moment in the story: What's the worst that can happen right here? That's what you should make happen!

Comedic Character Builder

Try to make 30 tertiary connections in order to write great comedic characters who will solve their problem in any way BUT the way they should.

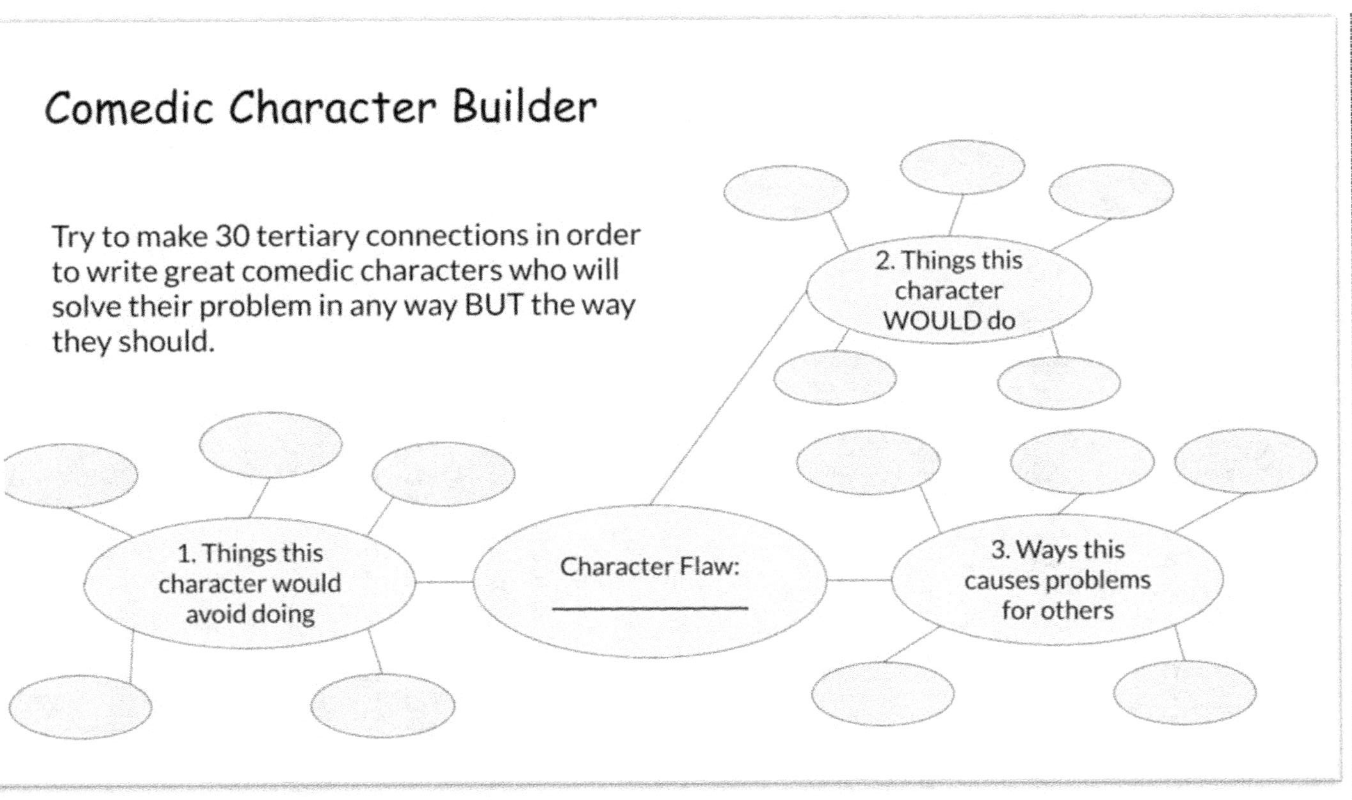

People don't watch drama to see characters make good choices. Often, the choice we know they *should* make is not the one they *do* make. Let your characters make mistakes and deal with the outcomes of their actions.

Comic Premise

Another small difference between comedy and drama is the **Comic Premise**. Premise is what the story is about. If a friend asks you what your play is about and you answer in 1-2 sentences - that's your premise.

Imagine:

- (Bruce Almighty) A regular guy gets the powers of God for a week.
- (School of Rock) An unemployed musician pretends to be a substitute teacher and turns his class into a rock band.
- (Groundhog Day) A man is stuck reliving Groundhog Day over and over again.
- (Freaky Friday) A mother and daughter magically switch bodies and must navigate each other's lives while trying to find a way back to normal.
- (Night at the Museum) A security guard at a museum has to contain all the exhibits as they come to life at night.

A great comic premise is either impossible or incredibly unlikely to happen in real life. But, in your story, it *does* happen, and now we discover what happens to your characters along the way.

A great comic premise excites you and has the plot of the play stirring in your head from the moment you discover the premise.

To discover your premise, here are some things you can do if you're struggling:

- Take any normal, average character.
- Brainstorm a list of 10 or more things that are the most unimaginable things that could happen to that person.
- As you brainstorm, return to your character tree. Use these scenarios to poke at their goals, fears, and flaws.
- Go for wacky and wild. "Death" is unimaginable for a person, but usually not interesting or funny. "Death of a beloved lizard" could be a bit more interesting.
- Choose one from your list that excites you with possibilities or one that puts your character in situations they don't know how to handle.

Once you make your choice, raise the stakes. Any problem your character has should be both **important** to solve and **hard** to solve.

How to write your premise really well

Think back to your thematic question. A great comic premise is another way to illustrate your thematic argument.

Think back to your character tree. A great comic premise gives you plenty of opportunities to press on your character's fears and their flaws.

Scenes

Plot is the overall roadmap of your story. Scenes are the words on the page, the actual events that happen. If plot is the roadmap, scenes are the turn-by-turn directions.

What happens in the scene moves your plot forward and causes change to your character.

Write a scene well, and your audience can't look away. Write a scene poorly, and your audience checks their phones while you waste paper.

You don't need to write your entire play in order scene-by-scene. Sometimes, a great scene, a great moment, a great beat pops into your head and you just need to write it down before it leaves you. That's okay! Write it down and keep it somewhere. Plug it into your play when it works.

Don't become too attached to a scene that you're afraid to cut it or revise it. As a writer friend once told me, "Don't get married to anything too early." I can't tell you the number of times my finger has hovered over the *delete* key, trembling in fear because a scene I love just isn't working in the overall story. However, every time I have deleted scenes (or sometimes entire acts) that aren't working, I have *always* ended up with something better.

Scene Tip 1: Enter late, leave early

Setting: Coffee shop.

BOB: Hey.

JERRY: Hey.

BOB: What ya' doing?

JERRY: Getting coffee. What you doing?

BOB: Getting coffee.

JERRY: Cool.

BOB: Yeah. Hey, what happened to that ten bucks I loaned you?

JERRY: You never loaned me ten dollars!

Most of that scene didn't need to happen. This writer (definitely not me) could have opened this scene right at, "You never loaned me ten dollars!"

Your audience can infer a lot of information without being directly told. When your audience sees the characters on the coffee shop set, we can tell they're getting coffee without anyone saying anything. If they get through the scene and halfway through, the barista hands them coffee, then we can assume they already ordered.

Start at "You never loaned me ten dollars!" and we can assume Bob just asked him about that. We can also tell they know each other, so we don't need to see them say, "Hey" when they enter.

Enter your scene at the latest possible point where we can still understand what's happening. Likewise, leave your scene at the earliest possible point. Unless it's essential to the plot that we see Jerry and Bob say goodbye, such as if Jerry gets struck by lightning and Bob gets upset he'll never recover his ten dollars, then we don't need to see the exit.

Scene Tip 2: Intention, Obstacle, and Tactics

This advice comes from the award-winning screenwriter Aaron Sorkin, whose credits include <u>A Few Good Men</u>, <u>The West Wing</u>, <u>The Newsroom</u>, <u>The Social Network</u>, and more. You may have heard the famous line, "You can't handle the truth!" That's from <u>A Few Good Men</u>.

Sorkin says Intention and Obstacle are the basic building blocks of a scene. Someone wants something, and something is standing in their way. That may sound remarkably similar to plot, and it is. Intention and obstacle are important not just in the overall plot, but in an individual scene as well.

Let's examine this scene from <u>Toy Story</u>. Read it twice. On the first read, just familiarize yourself with it. On the second read, try to figure out 1) Who wants what? 2) What is standing in their way?

Buzz: According to my Naval Computer, the...

Woody: Shut up! Just shut up, you idiot!

Buzz: Sheriff, this is no time to panic.

Woody: This is the perfect time to panic! I'm lost, Andy is gone, they're gonna move house in two days and it's all your fault!!

Buzz: My... my fault? If you hadn't pushed me out of the window in the first place...

Woody: Oh. Yeah. Well, if you hadn't showed up in your stupid little cardboard spaceship and taking away everything that was important to me...

Buzz: Don't talk to me about importance. And because of you, the security of this entire universe is in jeopardy.

Woody: WHAT?! What are you talking about?

Buzz: Right now, at the edge of the galaxy, Emperor Zurg has built a weapon with a secret capacity to annihilate an entire planet. I alone have information that reveals his weapons systems. And you, my friend, are responsible for delaying my rendezvous with Star Command!

Woody: (screaming with rage) YOU...ARE...A...TOY!!! You aren't the real Buzz Lightyear, you're an... aw, you're an action FIGURE! You are a child's... plaything!

BUZZ: And you are a sad, strange little man. Good luck to you, and farewell.

In this scene, Buzz wants to rendezvous with Star Command, and this crazy little sheriff is standing in his way. But, Woody also wants something: to get back to Andy, and put Buzz in his place as a toy beneath Woody in the social standing of Andy's toys.

In this scene, did either of them get what they want? No! But they clearly want *something* and they try to get it.

A scene where nobody wants anything is not a story. A scene where people want something but they don't try to get it is dull and uninteresting. Further, it's usually not just one person who wants something; multiple people want something, and often, their conflicting wants get in each other's way.

How do they go about getting what they want? That, according to Sorkin, is their *tactics*. How they get what they want reveals their character; it reveals who they are.

Woody tries to get what he wants by shouting over Buzz. Earlier, he tried to get rid of Buzz by pushing him out a window. Those actions - *tactics* - say a great deal about who Woody is - that he considers himself both in charge and Andy's favorite, and he won't tolerate being bumped off the top spot.

Buzz, on the other hand, truly believes he is the real Buzz Lightyear on a mission from Star Command. No matter what Woody tells him, he digs in, intent on fulfilling his mission to rescue the galaxy from Zurg.

As you begin your scene, start with a clear understanding of who wants what? What sorts of things are they willing to do to get it?

Scene Tip 3: Stakes

Aaron Sorkin is my favorite writer, and David Mamet is Sorkin's favorite writer, so it makes sense to include some wisdom from Mamet.

Mamet's wisdom here builds a bit off Sorkin. According to Mamet, every scene should answer three questions:

1. Who wants what?
2. What happens if they don't get it?
3. Why now?

This is what we call the *stakes*: why is it important for your characters to get what they want *now*?

In one of my earliest plays, set in the late 1800s, two swindlers were conning their way across the country to San Francisco. However, as I began revising, I realized I had a problem: the stakes weren't high enough. Obviously, they wanted to get to San Francisco, but why? And why now?

When I rewrote it, I added a plot point that one character's mom, who lived in San Francisco, was dying. This character ran away years ago on bad terms and wanted to make it back to make things right with her mom before she died.

Adding that point checked off Mamet's points 2 and 3, and raised the stakes considerably and showed us why these characters *had* to be successful.

In the original <u>Star Wars</u>, now known as <u>Episode IV: A New Hope</u>, the Rebels race to destroy the Death Star before it comes within range of destroying their base. But, in the original draft of the script (and even in the draft they used to shoot the movie), the Death Star was not closing in on destroying the Rebel base! It was just sitting out in the middle of space, and the Rebels conducted a sneak attack.

As the editing team cut the film together, they realized this lacked tension - it lacked *stakes*. If the Rebels failed, so what? Through creative editing, they changed the plot to make the Death Star closing down on the Rebel base, armed and ready to destroy it the moment it was within range. Now, if the Rebels failed to destroy the Death Star *right now,* not only would they fail, but the entire Rebellion would die in a single shot.

Adding that plotline satisfied the *why now* requirement and added plenty of dramatic tension to the audience. As you study other films, plays, and books, break it down and try to study Mamet's three questions, particularly *why now?*

- <u>Cars</u>: Lightning McQueen must repair the damage he caused to Radiator Springs so that he can go win the Piston Cup *this weekend!*
- <u>Finding Nemo</u>: Nemo is in *imminent danger* after being kidnapped, so Marlin immediately takes off to rescue him!
- <u>Toy Story</u>: Buzz and Woody need to get back to Andy because he's moving in *only a few days!*

<u>Scene Tip 4: Raise the Stakes</u>

This, I learned from doing improv comedy, in which actors make up (improvise) entire scenes off the top of their heads based only on limited suggestions from the audience (like the TV show <u>Whose Line is it Anyway</u>).

My improv teacher taught us to understand our goal in a scene right away, and to understand what makes the goal important. Then, as we go along in the scene (which may last 5ish minutes, where we're making it all up as we go along), we keep making things happen that make the goal even *more important* and even *more difficult* to obtain.

That is how you raise the stakes as you build scenes on top of each other. Every scene needs to *move* the story along, but how? You either get your hero even closer to their goal, or you do something to make the goal even *more important* to reach, or something that makes the goal *harder* to reach. Let's again look at <u>Cars</u>:

Lightning McQueen's goal is to repair the damage he did to Radiator Springs so he can make it to the Piston Cup. Along the way, he:

- Becomes friends with Mater, and gains the sense that he can't let his friends down (more important).
- Learns the history of Radiator Springs, and how the people there are trying to hold on to what was once a proud, important town (more important).
- Doc Hudson, afraid of McQueen becoming a bad influence, calls the racing paparazzi to run him out of town (more difficult).

In my personal favorite film <u>Back to the Future</u>, Marty McFly accidentally time travels from 1985 to 1955 without the plutonium power source he needs to return.

- Marty can't get plutonium in 1955 (more difficult).
- Marty interfered with his parents' first meeting, putting his own existence in jeopardy (more difficult).
- Marty discovers that his siblings are being erased from existence, and he needs to get his parents together before he himself is erased from existence (more important).
- Marty's mom Lorraine is not at all interested in his dad George (more difficult).
- Biff keeps getting in the way and interrupting Marty's attempts to get his parents together (more difficult).

- Marty must get his parents together before trying to leave 1955 (more important).

The purpose of scenes is to move your plot forward by causing changes to your character. Raising the stakes by making their goal more important or more difficult causes your character to take actions to reach their goal.

A scene that does not move your character closer to their goal or raise the stakes in some way has no point in existing. If you have one of these pointless scenes, you will likely find that you can cut it completely with no impact on the overall story. If, for some reason, you absolutely can't let it go because it contains important information, then add to it an event that raises the stakes.

Scene Tip 5: Be Interesting

This should go without saying, but I will say it anyway: You must *try* to be interesting. Very few writers are so magic that every word that comes out of their fingertips is so interesting that it causes readers and audiences to swoon. No, most writers, in order to be interesting, need to *try*.

Before you start writing a scene, brainstorm *at least* three different ways it could begin. Usually, the first way you come up with will be the least interesting. The more ideas you generate, the harder each idea will be to come up with, but the more interesting they will be. Once you have an idea, write it down, but then put it aside and try to think of something completely different.

Alex Osborn was a psychologist who studied how people become creative. He wanted to know what was going on inside the brains of creative people. A key discovery of his is this: *Quantity breeds quality.*

More ideas make more good ideas. The more ideas you generate, the more likely you are to have good ones. Sometimes, in order to have one really good idea, you need to fight through fifty so-so ideas.

Therefore, don't start writing a scene until you have envisioned several ways the scene could go. What would be interesting to your audience? What would be delightfully surprising? What would hook them in and make them *need* to see what comes next?

Further, don't just do this for the beginning of the scene. Ask yourself, "What's the most surprising thing that could happen in this scene?" Do the same sort of idea generation. Remember: audiences want to be *delightfully* surprised. They want to think they know what's coming next, and then be surprised with something better.

Few writers can be interesting without trying. For you, you will need to *try* to be interesting.

The composer Mozart wrote entire pieces of music entirely in his head and they were perfect the first time he wrote them down. Beethoven, on the other hand, had draft manuscripts filled with scribbles, crossouts, erasures, grunts, notes, and additions. Beethoven's manuscripts made it clear he had to work things out as he wrote.

It's okay to be like Beethoven. Most people are like Beethoven.

Dialogue

Dialogue Tip 1: Subtext

Dialogue is what people say, the actual words of your scene. Every book on writing you will ever read will say something like, "Don't let your dialogue be too on-the-nose. Let your dialogue have subtext."

If you are anything like me, you won't have the foggiest idea what that means no matter how hard the authors work to explain it to you. It took me too long to understand what subtext is, how to explain it, and how to write it. But, after years of failing, I now have a strong enough grasp to explain it to you! (Insert my own back-patting here.)

Imagine this: A friend calls. They aren't calling for any particular reason; they just want to chat. You, however, don't want to chat. You're not in the mood for talking. You just want to hang up.

Your problem is, you don't want to hurt their feelings. So, do you say something like, "Hey, I really don't want to talk right now. Can we call later?"

If you would, you're a better person than 99% of the people I know, including me. No, what most people I know would do is say something like, "Hey, I was just about to lay down to take a nap" (even though you're gearing up for a long round of video games). Then, it's your friend who apologizes to *you* and hangs up!

Yes, you lied to your friend. Hate to break it to you, but if you're going to be a writer, you need to be a keen observer of human behavior and *humans lie all the darn time!*

What you really wanted to say was, "I don't want to talk to you right now." But what you actually said was, "I was about to take a nap."

Let me put it this way: The *dialogue* was, "I was about to take a nap," but the *subtext* was, "I don't want to talk to you right now."

Subtext is what a character wants to say but doesn't. Sometimes they're trying to protect feelings, sometimes they are too scared to say it, sometimes they don't want to admit it. Truth is, humans *rarely* say exactly what we *want* to say. Most of the time we dance around the issue, saying other things to avoid it.

Take this example from <u>Cars</u>:

> **Harv:** Listen, they're giving you 20 tickets for the tiebreaker thing in Cali. I'll pass 'em on to your friends. You shoot me the names. You let Harv rock it for you, alright, baby?
>
> **Lightning McQueen:** Right! Friends! Yes, there's, um… (silence)

Lightning wasn't going to say, "I don't think I have any true friends, Harv." But, from his silence, we get the idea.

Or a simple example from <u>Toy Story</u>:

> **Buzz:** I'll set my phaser to stun.
>
> **Woody:** Great. We'll blink 'em to death.

What did Woody want to say there? Probably something like, "Buzz, what have I been trying to say? You're just a toy! That's not a real laser!"

Not every line of dialogue needs subtext. Subtext happens when there's a difference between what the character wants and what they want to express. Artful use of subtext is what makes audiences go, "Wow, this writer's good."

To write subtext well:

1. Look for a place where you did write exactly what the character wanted to say. Then,
2. Ask yourself, "Is there a more artful way of doing this?"

You can do this artfully by:

- Let the character lie.
- Let the character bite their tongue and not say anything at all.
- Have the character change the subject.
- Make a joke instead.

You can only do this well if you truly understand what your character wants and what is keeping your character from getting it, both in the overall story and in this scene specifically.

In the case of Woody and Buzz, Woody's frustration with Buzz leads to him being sarcastic instead of honest. In the case of Lightning McQueen, Lightning's self-consciousness and unwillingness to admit his faults make him... you know, not.

In the case of our hypothetical friend from the beginning of this chapter, our desire to protect their feelings causes us to lie.

You don't always need to cover up your character's true intentions. But, it's good to find places where doing so adds depth to the story or to the characters.

It's good to do so in ways that make your characters more interesting.

Dialogue Tip 2: Don't write how people actually talk

This is the tip that could get me in some trouble. I've seen many script reviewers give feedback that says, "People don't really sound like that" as if that were a goal we're shooting for. But, if you watch a movie or a play, how many characters do we see talk the way people actually talk in real life? I would be hard pressed to see many of the dramatic conversations we see on film or stage actually play out between real people.

I'm not saying we need to go full Shakespearian - *"But soft! What light beyond thy yonder window breaks? It is the east, and Juliet is the sun!"*

No, but what I am saying is we spend all day listening to people talk in real life. When we see a drama, we want to see *better*.

This is why I appreciate writers like Aaron Sorkin. His characters sound like I imagine I would sound if I got ten minutes to plan every line I said. His characters sound the way I *want* to sound. Take this dialogue from an episode of <u>The West Wing</u> between President Bartlett and one of his advisors, Josh Lyman:

Josh: Uh, long story short - you're going to be reading a bit today about your secret plan to fight inflation.

President: I have a secret plan to fight inflation?

Josh: No.

President: Why am I going to be reading that I do?

Josh: It was suggested in the press room that you did.

President: By who?

Josh: By me.

President: You told the press I have a secret plan to fight inflation?

Josh: No, I did not. Let me be absolutely clear I did not do that! Except yes, I did that.

President: Josh, I'm a little confused.

Josh: Sir, there was this idiotic round robin. It was sarcastic! There's no way they didn't know that. They were just mad at me for imposing discipline and calling them stupid!

President: A secret plan to fight inflation?

Josh: There was no turning it back. I denied it for half an hour!

President: Were you clear?

Josh: I was crystal clear! They asked, "Do you think if the president has a plan to fight inflation that it's right to keep it a secret?" I said, "Of course not!"

President: Are you telling me that not only did you invent a secret plan to fight inflation, but now you don't support it?

Josh: (Struggling to find something to say) When
you put it like that, Mr. President…

Bottom line: Have fun with your dialogue. Make it
something that is delightful to read and delightful for
actors to perform. That will make it delightful to listen
to. Don't try to make it real.

Many modern presidents have had tape recording
systems in the Oval Office, and we can listen to
recordings of their meetings at their presidential
libraries. So many of these recordings are so
incredibly boring to listen to, while the movie versions
of these conversations are fascinating. People don't
want real life; they want better. Be better than real life.
Have fun.

Dialogue Tip 3: You have two pages for us to get your character

The way characters are introduced says a great
deal about who they are. In reality, you have about
two pages for us to know everything we need to know
about that character.

This is the dialogue chapter, but often, you don't
even need dialogue. In <u>Pirates of the Caribbean,</u>
Captain Jack Sparrow is introduced with a series of
shots:

- Standing tall at the top of a mast on his ship.

- He grabs a rope and rappels down to the deck, where his grand ship is revealed to be a tiny dinghy.
- His dinghy is sinking as he bails water out.
- He stops bailing water to salute several hung pirates.
- His dinghy finally sinks at the perfect time for him to step right off the top mast onto the dock.
- And then, with a bit of dialogue, he bribes the dock official to not record his name in the log book.

There. In under two pages, we know everything we need to know about Captain Jack Sparrow. Yes, we will learn more throughout the story, but everything we *need* to know shows up right here: he's a pirate, perhaps not the best sailor, and of dubious morals.

As Buzz Lightyear is dropped off on Andy's bed, we see him cautiously wander the surface, reporting his observations back to Star Command. This tells us everything we need to know: Buzz actually thinks he's the real Buzz Lightyear.

When you introduce your characters, get to it! Show us who they are. Remember Sorkin's *intention, obstacle,* and *tactics*? Show us those tactics right away, in their first two pages.

Dialogue Tip 4: Dialogue is Character

Inexperienced writers use dialogue to inform the audience about what is going on. We hear characters say things like, "Okay, the plan is..." "I think we should do..." etc.

Artful writers use dialogue to reveal character. Dialogue helps us discover who the characters are.

This is what happens in <u>Pirates of the Caribbean</u> whenever someone refers to Jack Sparrow and he corrects them by adding, "*Captain* Jack Sparrow." It's part of Jack's character that he needs people to know his status - he's a *Captain!*

Some interpret this as meaning that dialogue can never reveal plot information. That is not true. It means that if the only purpose of a section of dialogue is to reveal plot information, then it's not an artful way of telling the story.

Let's examine this scene from <u>Toy Story.</u> It may seem like the only purpose is to convey plot information, but I would like to argue it has a deeper purpose:

                 WOODY
Hello? Check? Better? Great.
Everybody hear me? Up on the
shelf, can you hear me? Great!
Okay, first item today...oh, yeah.
Has everyone picked a moving buddy?

The toys all MOAN.

                    HAMM
Moving buddy?! You can't be serious!

                    REX
Well I didn't know we were supposed
to have one already.

              MR. POTATO HEAD
              (waving his arm out
               its socket)
Do we have to hold hands?

The toys LAUGH and SNICKER.

                   WOODY
Oh, yeah, you guys think this is a
big joke. We've only got one week
left before the move. I don't want
any toys left behind. A moving
buddy -- if you don't have one, get
one!
         (checking the pad)
Alright, next...uh...oh, yes.
Tuesday night's "Plastic Corrosion
Awareness" meeting was, I think, a
big success and we want to thank Mr.
Spell for putting that on for us.
Thank you, Mr. Spell.

The words "You're welcome" scroll across Mr. Spell's display
screen as he speaks.

                 MR. SPELL
You're welcome.

                  WOODY
Ok, uh...oh yes. One minor note
here...

> (under his breath)
> Andy's birthday party's been moved
> to today.
>> (full voice)
> Next we have --

The toys all PANIC.

> REX
> What?! Whadda ya mean, the party's
> today?! His birthday's not 'til
> next week!!

> HAMM
> What's going on down there? Is Mom
> losing her marbles?!

> WOODY
> Well, obviously she wanted to have
> the party before the move. I'm not
> worried. You shouldn't be worried.

> MR. POTATO HEAD
> Of course Woody ain't worried!
> He's been Andy's favorite since
> kindergarten!

Is plot information being conveyed here? Yes, absolutely. We are learning that Woody is in charge, he's Andy's favorite, Andy is moving in the next few days, and birthday parties are worrisome affairs for Andy's toys.

But we are also learning about Woody's character: he sees himself as in charge, and the other toys see him as in charge. He sees it as his responsibility to take care of the rest of the toys and, in a way, Andy as well. This sets us up nicely for later, when Buzz seems to upset Woody's place as the "favorite toy." Being the leader is a core part of Woody's character that will have serious implications if challenged.

Dialogue and staged actions are the only two ways of conveying plot information. However, use dialogue to convey *who* these people are and *how* they think, not just what is happening.

Read this scene from my own <u>Real Fakes: The True Story of the Fake Spy who Saved D-Day.</u> This scene serves as the introduction to two characters - Tommy and Sarah, who work for the British Intelligence Agency in World War II.

After you read, remember *Intention, Obstacle, Tactics:* list everything you know about who these two are and how they go about solving problems.

SCENE 4 - "THE SNAKEPIT" - BRITISH MILITARY INTEL. HQ.

TOMMY HARRIS stands in a dingy basement of British Military Intelligence. He has a pile of reports and papers on his desk, but stands facing a classical painting on an easel, studying it. He's in his early 30s, half-Jewish, is sometimes called "Jesus" by his friends due to his passing resemblance to the way Jesus is depicted in Renaissance art. Before joining MI5, he was an art dealer. On a table behind him, a mysterious object is covered under a sheet.

SARAH BISHOP enters with some coffee. She puts it on his desk, startling him.

SARAH. Mister Harris?

TOMMY. Shhh...

SARAH. Mister -

TOMMY. Shhh!

SARAH. Does the painting need quiet?

TOMMY. Look at the lighting on this. Isn't it fantastic?

SARAH. It's a painting.

TOMMY. Two hundred pounds at auction, easy. I've been trying to get my hands on this since before the war. *(They stand for a moment.)* Who are you?

SARAH. I'm Sarah Bishop. I work for you. As an analyst.

TOMMY. No you don't.

SARAH. I started yester- no, today! Today's my first day.

TOMMY. Who hired you?

SARAH. Colonel Robinson.

TOMMY. Ha!

SARAH. Where's today's parcel? I should start going through it.

TOMMY. I know you. Where do you really work?

SARAH. Right here. Oh, hey, your log books! I know how these work. *(catches herself)* Because... I work here, obviously.

TOMMY. As an analyst.

SARAH. Yes.

TOMMY. You're one of the secretaries in the transcription pool!

SARAH. I'm an analyst. I start today.

TOMMY. Under whose authority?

SARAH. Colonel Robinson.

TOMMY. Ha!

SARAH. Mister Harris-

TOMMY. Tommy.

SARAH. Tommy. I'm wasted as a transcriptionist. I can do more.

TOMMY. Colonel Robinson would get his knockers in a twist if I promoted a woman.

SARAH. How's the war going?

TOMMY. *(smiles, reaches into a satchel, and pulls out a piece of paper. He hands it to Sarah.)* Okay, Analyst Bishop. Analyze. *(She reads the paper.)* The Franco government in Spain. They're neutral. But will they stay neutral?

SARAH. Hitler helped Franco win the Spanish Civil War.

TOMMY. Indeed.

SARAH. But Spain is still in shambles. And they rely too much on imports from the United States.

TOMMY. How do we get them to stay neutral?

> **SARAH.** *(thinking aloud)* They can't push back an Allied invasion, and Germany can't defend France AND Spain. Send chatter that Spain is the perfect place to gain a land foothold if they join the war.
>
> **TOMMY.** *(takes a sip of coffee.)* Make sure Colonel Robinson knows you're grateful we're not in the trenches.
>
> **SARAH.** *(slightly confused)* Sir? Trenches were the last war.
>
> **TOMMY.** Get used to it, 'cause that's where Colonel Robinson's head is.

Yes, much plot information is relayed in that scene giving us background information about the war. However, how do Sarah and Tommy go about pursuing their goals? What are the *tactics* they use to get what they want?

Sarah knew she was up to the job and didn't wait for anyone's permission; she simply walked in and declared herself an analyst, lying to Tommy until he accepted her.

And Tommy is an art dealer who doesn't seem too fond of his boss, Colonel Robinson. Therefore, while he knows Robinson would not have hired a woman, Tommy is willing to give her a chance if she can prove she's up to the job. He likely does not have too much respect for proper protocol.

While that scene tells us a great deal about what is happening in the story, it also tells us about who they are. This is why your character tree becomes so important - knowing their right leg actions and their left leg actions and the things that they *do* to solve problems gives you a great place from which to drive your dialogue.

Jokes

You don't need to be the quickest-witted, funniest person to write jokes. You just need to understand how jokes work!

The part of a joke that makes people laugh is called the **punch line**. Take these examples:

I used to work at a calendar factory, but I got fired. **They said I took too many days off.**

Why couldn't the bicycle stand up? **It was two-tired.**

I made a pencil with two erasers. **It was pointless.**

Punchlines make people laugh when we make the audience expect one thing, and give them something else instead.

Here's a joke from my own <u>Not a Murder Mystery.</u>

> **MELINDA.** Anyone who's not a millionaire is simply too lazy to become one. All it takes is some hard work, grit, and a good idea.
>
> **HARPER.** How'd you become a millionaire?
>
> **MELINDA.** My father died.

I lured you into a false sense of security. Here's Melinda, preaching about becoming a millionaire through hard work. When you ask her how she became rich, you expect a rags-to-riches tale about persisting through long odds when no one believed in her in order to market a game-changing invention. But no, she just inherited millions from her rich father.

Here are two good ways of creating unexpected punchlines:

Joke Technique 1: Shifting

To write a joke, understand that every story has a *Who, What, When, Where, Why,* and *How.* But, some of those we **know** from the dialogue, and other bits we **assume** we know without being told. Take this setup:

"I gave my cat a bath the other day… they love it! He sat there. He enjoyed it. It was fun for me, too!"

Here's what we **know** from that setup:

Who: Me and my cat.
What: A bath.
When: The other day.

The others you don't know, but you can **assume** you know based on your knowledge of how baths work:

Where: In the bathtub.
Why: The cat is dirty.
How: Washing with soap and water.

The key here is you don't actually know those things. They are not stated in the story! But, most people being reasonable people who know how baths work will picture those assumptions in their heads.

To make a joke, flip one of the **assumptions** into something else. For example, flip the *How*. Now, here's the entire joke:

"I gave my cat a bath the other day… they love it! He sat there. He enjoyed it. It was fun for me, too!

Everything except the part where his fur kept sticking to my tongue."

That's called a *how-shift*. I never actually said how I was giving my cat a bath.

To do the shifting technique, have a character's dialogue tell a story where some of the *Who, What, When, Where, Why,* and *How* is explicitly stated, and some of those facts are only assumed. Then, change one of the assumptions into something else.

Here's another example I'm making up right now for the purpose of this book:

LINDA: We acted our hearts out in that scene! I can't believe the audience booed us!

TERRI: And the rest of the cast, too. Gee, talk about cooperation.

NAIOMI: You… you guys weren't even in the play. You jumped onto the stage from the front row! You pretty much ruined it for everyone.

LINDA: I guess some people just don't know talent!

Let's break that down again from the first two lines, between Linda and Terri. What do we **know**?

Who: Linda and Terri.
What: Acting in a performance.
When: Recently.
Where: On stage.

We don't know these details for sure, but before Naiomi speaks, we **assume** these two details:

Why: They're in the cast.
How: Acting poorly.

I use Naiomi's line to *why-shift*: we assume they're in the cast, but I reveal here that they were just two audience members who jumped up on stage! Had I started with Naiomi's line, it wouldn't have been a joke. What makes it a joke is the way I set it up for you to *expect* that they were just bad actors, and then delivered something else.

Joke Technique 2: The Reversal

This uses the same philosophy as the shifting technique: setting up the audience to expect one thing and then delivering something else. In fact, my earlier example of Millionaire Melinda inheriting her millions was an example of just this.

Here's another example:

> **CRAIG:** Hey! You can't just buy me like that? I have morals!
>
> **LARRY:** $25,000?
>
> **CRAIG:** I think you just bought me.

One more example, from <u>Pirates of the Caribbean:</u>

> **JACK:** This girl, how far are you willing to go to save her?
>
> **WILL:** I'd die for her.
>
> **JACK:** Well, good then.

What makes a good reversal funny is when there's a mismatch between who the character *says* they are and who they *actually* are, as revealed by their actions. The reversals by Millionaire Melinda and between Craig and Larry are examples of this: their first lines set up an expectation of who they say they are, and their second lines reveal who they actually are.

Now, this doesn't need to happen all the time, such as in the Jack Sparrow example. It simply delights the audience when they are led to expect one thing, and then get something else.

Dialogue Exercise

Find a completely random picture.

Write a two-minute scene between two characters that is somehow related to this picture.

Remember *tactics:* these two characters should be two completely different people who think and talk and problem-solve in completely different ways.

When you're finished, delete the names. Show it to a friend with only the dialogue. Can your friend tell who is who based on the character's tactics?

Finding your Voice

Earlier in this book, I very rudely stated that you are nobody. While that may be true now, I hope it is not true very soon. Truly and sincerely - I wrote this book to enable you to be successful and achieve your dreams. Right now, I may have never heard of you. However, as a fellow dreamer who wants everyone who dreams to be able to achieve those dreams, perhaps you will be one of my favorite writers someday soon.

In order to do that, you need to be *you*. You need to be *uniquely* you. Find a way of speaking, a way of telling your stories, that makes people who read or see your works instantly recognize it as one of yours.

Taylor Swift and Luke Combs both play guitar, and both sound uniquely different from each other. John Legend and the Beatles both sing, and both sound uniquely different from each other. If singers and musical artists can have their own unique voice or style, so can writers. You can recognize a Dr. Seuss book or a Roald Dahl book within a few pages.

Maybe, they do it through the dialogue. Aaron Sorkin has a way of writing dialogue that is witty, snappy, and unique to him in a way few other writers can pull off. To Sorkin, dialogue is like music - it has rhythm, tempo, pitch, and a melody. Watch a few Sorkin productions and you'll begin to recognize a Sorkin production when you see one.

Maybe it's through your structure. Christopher Lloyd was a producer and writer on the TV show <u>Frasier</u> (not to be confused with the actor Christopher Lloyd who played Doc in <u>Back to the Future</u>, who I spent years too long not realizing was a different person entirely). <u>Frasier</u> is a master of the *farce*, a comedy style built on lies, misunderstandings, and heightened comedic scenarios. Lloyd brings his unique understanding of how to structure a farce to so many of Frasier's best episodes, it's easy to recognize it's him.

Likewise, playwright Ken Ludwig brings a similar taste in farce to the stage in plays like <u>Lend Me a Tenor,</u> <u>Moon Over Buffalo</u>, <u>Leading Ladies</u>, and <u>Shakespeare in Hollywood</u>.

Maybe it's through your views on life. TV writer Michael Shur's credits include <u>The Office</u>, <u>Parks and Rec</u>, <u>The Good Place</u>, and <u>Brooklyn Nine-Nine</u>. These shows are mostly workplace comedies involving normal people confronting abnormal situations, but always make you wonder, "What does it mean to do the right thing?" Most of Shur's best episodes of these series involve characters confronted with impossible choices or situations, and their struggle to find the right response challenges the audience to wonder, "How do we know what the right thing may be?"

Maybe it's how you personalize big issues. In her plays <u>Radium Girls</u>, <u>A Thing of Beauty,</u> and <u>The Other American</u>, DW Gregory is able to take big, abstract political issues and show how they impact the lives of ordinary people. You will feel for her characters, often the "little guy" fighting against far more powerful interests.

Finding your own voice is hard. If you have a moment, hop on YouTube and find a video of Jimmy Hendrix performing the Star Spangled Banner.

When you hear this rendition of the National Anthem, realize this: no one taught Jimmy Hendrix to play this way. He probably took guitar lessons (I don't know for sure), but no one ever taught him *that*. He figured that out on his own.

As a writer trying to find your voice, no one can teach you how with any degree of certainty. I can, however, recommend a few exercises to help you explore who you are and what you sound like.

Voice Tip 1: Analyze your favorite writers

Find your favorite writers and read multiple examples of their works. Understand who they are, what makes them tick, and how this comes across in their writing.

Imagine their dialogue as music, and the characters as instruments. What instruments do they like to use? What sounds do they use over and over again? What's their rhythm?

Understanding other writers, over time, will give you insight into your own style. Seek out writers who have their own distinctive voice. Notice, when you read anything, the writers that stand out as having a unique sound, style, and voice.

Write out full descriptions of *why* you like this writer's style. Be thorough and complete. Here are two examples of some of my favorite writers:

"I really like the style of Aaron Sorkin. He doesn't write what people really sound like, he writes a better version of them. His characters always talk the way I want to talk. They all sound as smart as I would sound if I got ten minutes to plan everything I got to say."

"Bill Bryson sounds whimsical. I like his train of connected thoughts in his run-on sentences. He uses sarcasm that isn't over the top, but draws attention to odd observations about everyday things."

Voice Tip 2: Understand what makes you... you!

Are you beginning to realize that I love doing word bubbles? Exploring these connections helps your creative brain come to life!

Here, I have not one word bubble, but SIX! Come up with as many connections as you can to these six things:

- Your typical mood
- Life events that shape you

- Your personality - according to you
- Your personality - according to others
- Core beliefs
- Core dislikes or frustrations

Find secondary and tertiary connections as well. Work on defining and understanding yourself, what you care about, and what moves you, and that will show in your writing.

Voice Top 3: Understand Figurative Language

In the film <u>V for Vendetta</u>, one main character, who we learn to call only "V," introduces himself with a several minute long monologue in which nearly every word starts with a "v."

"Voila, in view, a humble vaudevillian veteran, cast vicariously as both victim and villain by the vicissitudes of fate. This visage, no mere veneer of vanity, is a vestige of the vox populi, now vacant, vanished..."

Literary devices and figurative language helps to make your writing more interesting, quirky, and artful. Understand these ten at minimum, and write examples of each:

- **Metaphor**: Compares two different things. *Jim is a giraffe. Life is a rollercoaster.*
- **Simile**: Compares the common characteristics of two different things using "like" or "as." *Larry is as loud as a lion. Life has ups and downs like a rollercoaster.*
- **Onomatopoeia**: A word that sounds like what it describes. *Roar! Drip, drip, drip. Ding!*
- **Personification**: Assigning human qualities to something that isn't human. *The blanket embraced me with a warm hug.*
- **Idiom**: A group of words that have a different meaning from the literal meaning. *Break a leg! Piece of Cake!*
- **Alliteration**: Repeating the same letter or sound at the beginning of words. *This valorous visitation of a bygone vexation stands vivified!*
- **Assonance**: Repeating the same vowel sound in a sentence. *The rain in Spain falls mainly on the plain.*
- **Hyperbole**: An exaggerated statement. *That was a killer joke!*
- **Oxymoron**: A sentence or phrase with two opposite or contradicting words. *That chair is pretty ugly. The sea was insanely calm.*
- **Puns**: Humor from words that have double meanings. Time flies like an arrow, fruit flies like a banana. Straws are for suckers.

Becoming familiar with these and comfortable writing them makes them come up automatically in your writing, which will give your writing a unique ring to it.

Voice Tip 4: Write short bits

Write short stories or plays, only a few pages or a few minutes long. Make an explicit attempt to sound unique and interesting. Practice this by picking a random subject, or elaborate extensively in a random fact.

Better yet, pick a random fact or subject and write two *different* stories in two *contrasting* styles. Working to make the styles different helps you to understand style in itself. Then, as you write more serious, longer works, your ability to write in your style will come forward.

Heart

It's easy to get caught up in "What should I do?" and wanting to do it "right."

The truth is, writing that sticks with people doesn't do so because it's "right." The books people read over and over again, the plays they go to time and again, and the movies they memorize stick with people because they have **heart**.

Every good story, no matter what it's about, is about the **people**. The people are the most important part of any story. When we care about what happens to the people, we care about the story.

You, as a writer, have heart. I don't know anyone who desires to be a writer who doesn't believe they have something inside of them worth sharing with the world. When you find what that is, you can be successful.

I once had a theatre teacher tell me, "Middle school plays are for jokes and slapstick." But, I know that's not all. The heart of your show is what gives people a reason to do the show. It's what gives people a reason to come back the second and third night.

And generally, your character's heart won't be all that different from your own. It's hard to hide who you are.

Give your characters heart. Let them speak. Then, the audience will find something to love within them.

Revising

Revising is perhaps harder than writing the first draft in the first place! It took me a long time to even know what to look for when revising, other than, "What's bad?"

Once the first draft exists (which, as you recall, is the only thing the first draft really *needs* to do), you worked really hard on it! Why can't you just start sending it to theatre companies, directors, or entering it in contests?

Your first draft likely took *months* to write. A lot goes on in a writer's mind in a month. Characters and plots evolve, points get lost and forgotten. You may have just trudged along trying to get to the end of a scene.

Here are some things to look for to improve upon your first draft. Remember: I have never regretted deleting a scene that didn't work. You won't either.

Revision Tip 1: Character Trees

Your understanding of a character will likely change from when you first wrote their name to their final scene in the story. Go through and do a character tree based on your understanding of that character *at the end of the story*. Then, look at their dialogue and their actions: does it stay consistent through the story to who they are?

For example, I once wrote a short film that had a character named Chris. By the end of the story, I recognized him as a bit of a slacker who avoided hard work by nature. I solidified that with a character tree I wrote after writing the first draft.

In revising, I found a line of dialogue. One character gave an idea, and Chris replied, "I like it."

Now, understanding Chris' character better, I changed "I like it" to "That sounds hard." It was a simple, but important change to Chris' role overall. At first, I didn't really have a reason why Chris would or wouldn't like the plan. But, as Chris evolved, I realized that, though he may go along with the plan, he most certainly wouldn't like it.

You may have done character trees at the beginning of the writing process. Now that you have finished, do them again. Then, read your story for consistency. Do the characters act the way they should act, and be who they should be?

Revision Tip 2: Intention and Obstacle

Go through every scene. Write an outline on a piece of paper - Scene 1: Coffee shop, Scene 2: Apartment, Scene 3: Street, etc.

For each scene, answer these questions:

- Who are the characters, and what are their intentions? What are their obstacles? What are their tactics? (Sorkin's questions).
- Who wants what? What happens if they don't get it? Why now? (Mamet's questions).

If you can't answer these questions for at least the two main characters in the scene, that points to an issue with the scene.

But, don't just go adding in intention and obstacle willy-nilly. Connect it back to your theme. Make your intentions something your character needs to do in order to reach their goal, and make your obstacles force them to change in the right ways.

If you can't answer Sorkin's questions and Mamet's questions for a scene, that's a scene that should be revised or eliminated.

Revision Tip 3: Check for loose ends

Writing takes a long time, and your story may count in the 100+ page range. It's easy to bring up something at the beginning of the story, and then completely forget about it.

Re-read looking specifically for these loose ends. Otherwise, your audience will do this for you, and I can tell you from first hand experience it's embarrassing to say, "I was going to do something with that, but then I didn't."

Revision Tip 4: Describe your hero

You may have a vision of your hero in your head. But now, using *only what's on the page*, write out a full description of your hero - their wants and goals, struggles and frustrations, their tactics. Don't use what's in your head; use only what you have written on the page.

Every fact and sentence you write should be directly traceable back to a line in your story. If you have an idea in your head that you *can't* trace back to a line in your story, understand why it's in your head in the first place. Then, if it needs to be in your story, go back and revise.

But, don't just describe your hero once. Describe your hero twice: who they are at the beginning of the story, and who they are at the end. If your character changed and learned the lessons of the theme, there should be distinct differences.

If you don't see change in alignment with your thematic question, you likely have some major revisions in order. Go through your plot points and ensure the events that happen to them cause changes toward understanding the theme.

Revision Tip 5: Character Voice

Inexperienced writers often end up with characters who all sound alike. Remove the character name from the page and it's hard to tell who's actually speaking.

This is okay in your first draft, because you're often just trying to get through the scene. But, go back now and understand who they are and what they sound like. Do they use big words or small words? Do they sound bright or dumb? Are they hopeful or cynical? Do they believe in themselves or do they lack confidence? Do they have a constant need to sound better than others?

Habits of Creative People

It's a common myth that people are "born" creative. Creativity is a learned skill that can be improved with intentional practice. Here are a few things you can do to practice and improve your ability to be creative on-demand whenever you need to.

Creativity Habit 1: Word Web

Practicing making word webs helps your brain learn to make connections. The more you practice this, the easier it will be for your brain to jump from the main idea out to the tertiary connection – what I call the "creativity zone." Do this often, and practice.

Creativity Habit 2: Be Curious

The more you practice being curious, the more curious you become. Observe the world. Ask questions. Ask why things are the way they are. Ask how things would be different if one thing were changed.

Creativity Habit 3: Embrace Failure

Don't let a fear of failure keep you from making something great. Every great idea is built on top of a mountain of dead, so-so ideas. Everything you try that doesn't work teaches you something valuable for your next attempt. Every project you write that doesn't sell teaches you how to make a better one for next time.

Creativity Habit 4: Write Things Down

Have a way of writing down any idea that pops into your head at any time. Personally, I have a note in my phone I can bring up at any moment. Ideas tend to pop in at the worst times – certainly never when I'm actually *trying* to write. They come as I'm trying to sleep, as I'm taking a walk, or watching TV. Write them down when they happen and keep them for later.

Creativity Habit 5: Reserve Judgement

There is a time for generating ideas, and there is a time for deciding whether or not ideas are good. These two times DO NOT overlap. Keep them separate. Generate 20-30 ideas, and then pick the good ones and the keepers.

This is especially important when working as a group!

Final Thoughts

You're not nobody. You're inexperienced and unrecognized outside your immediate circle.

But I believe in you. We dreamers need to stick together. Too few people will believe in us as we begin our own hero's journey. That's why I wrote this book - if you have the heart to start, you can be successful with coaching and guidance.

I have not yet reached the climax of my own journey. In order to earn a paycheck, I have spent far more time teaching than writing. But I, like you, will keep writing.

Don't get discouraged. It takes a *long time* to learn to be good at this. But, for some of you who are simply overflowing with good stories, the drive to keep going will be irresistible.

And, someday, when you see your own play on stage or your own book in a reader's hands, that journey will have been worth it.

Take breaks when you need to. Keep picking up that pen.

Break a leg.

-David Dubczak

Liked <u>How to Write a Play?</u>
Activate your Genius Mode!

Genius isn't a birthright. It's a habit you can train.

Activate Your Genius Mode shows teens and tweens (and the adults who guide them) how to turn creativity from something you wait for into something you can **do on demand**. Drawing on brain science and proven psychology, this fast, practical guide teaches the three core skills every creative thinker masters:

- Divergent thinking to generate bold options
- Convergent thinking to choose the best ones
- Planning to turn ideas into real results

Inside you'll find:

- A **30-day Creativity Bootcamp** with bite-sized daily reps
- The **Creative Problem-Solving (CPS) process**, used by psychologists and innovators to get reliable ideas fast
- **Activities, worksheets, and stories** that make the science stick—and the practice fun
- Additional online free resources only for those who purchase the book, including printables, videos, lesson plans, and more.

You'll walk away able to beat blocks, make better decisions, and ship your best ideas—whether you're a student, teacher, parent, or professional problem-solver.

Creativity isn't something you're born with. It's something you build.

Open the book. Flip the switch. *Activate your Genius Mode.*

★ ★ ★ ★ ★ What Parents and Teachers Are Saying

Empowering, Entertaining, and Perfectly Designed for Tweens & Teens! "Activate Your Genius Mode is a creative powerhouse of a book that speaks directly to young minds in a way that's equal parts hilarious, encouraging, and deeply practical. David Dubczak has taken the science of creativity and transformed it into an engaging, digestible guide that feels like your favorite teacher mixed with your funniest uncle-backed by real neuroscience and a genuine understanding of what makes tweens and teens tick..."

YOU NEED THIS BOOK. "I have found another way to introduce convergent and divergent thinking with my kiddos. He provides a 30 day plan to get them thinking! I don't know about you but my kids want to have the "right" answer and have it now. They are not good at really thinking deeply and not using the shallow responses they have. They also will just say I don't know or that's all I can think of if a question is challenging... I feel this book will enable me to explain and get them to not be so afraid of giving a "dumb" answer... I loved this book and can NOT wait to use it in my classroom in just a few weeks!!"

Now available from Amazon, Barnes & Noble, or ask your favorite bookseller to order from Ingram. Discounts on classroom sets available at www.DavidDWriter.com

Not the Best, Not the Worst; Just What You're Stuck With

Your parents bought you this book, didn't they? Either that, or your teacher is forcing you to read it. I know this because, as a former teenage boy, I didn't buy myself books called Activate Your Genius Mode. Any money I did have burned a hole in my pocket and went straight toward buying that Gameboy Color (which, my Millennial is showing, I know you didn't buy either).

Whoever that "caring adult" in your life happens to be, they probably say things like, "You have so much potential," or "My kid's a genius," or "Lord help me if you lose one more homework assignment before you turn it in!" (A tendency to lose things is correlated with a natural divergent thinking ability, which is a good thing, as far as the topic of this book is concerned).

Someone who thinks you - you - either can be or already are a genius and bought you this book. So, do at least this much and stick with me through the first chapter. There are three things you need to understand about so-called "geniuses":

1. There are very, very few natural born geniuses.
2. Most people we consider today to be "geniuses" have a higher-than-average ability to generate and act on original ideas.

3. This is an ability that can be - and often is - *learned.*

There are very, very few natural born geniuses

Wolfgang Amadeus Mozart wrote his first musical composition at the age of five, learned to play instruments simply from watching other people play them a few times, once listened to a multi-part choir piece *one time* and then went home and transcribed it on paper *from memory*, and wrote complete symphonies entirely in his head before writing them down on paper mistake-free.

It's hard to argue Mozart was not a natural-born genius. If you are anything like Mozart, congratulations. Give this book to your less-interesting neighbor who could actually use it.

A natural-born genius on the level of Mozart is a once-in-a-century event. Mozart, Einstein, Newton, Picasso: all natural-born geniuses. However, even today's modern-day "geniuses," I can make the case are really *learned genius* instead of *natural-born genius.* People like Steve Jobs, Steven Spielberg, or Walt Disney didn't have childhoods much different from you or me or anyone else you know. Even Beethoven, whose career slightly overlapped with Mozart, was known for crossing out large sections, crumpling up paper of music he didn't like, and doing a lot of grunting while he worked things out. Genius? Sure. Natural-born? I'd argue not.

The point is this: There *are* a lot of geniuses in today's world. Once a century, someone like Mozart comes along. The rest of the time, genius is an acquired skill.

If you stick with me past chapter 1, you will learn this power. It's not a story the Jedi will tell you,[1] but I will. Expect, however, to be a lot more like Beethoven.

<u>Most people we consider today to be "geniuses" have a higher-than-average ability to generate and act on original ideas</u>

When you think of someone who is "creative," you may think of your art teacher, Mr. Beast,[2] or your friend who finds unique ways to hide candy from your teacher.

People become famous for their creativity. Singers, authors, YouTubers, painters, graffiti artists, slam poets, hairstylists (the kind that think lip rings compliment blue hair), big tech CEOs, and the guy or gal who somehow made "skibidi" something people talk about. We then talk about their "creative genius."

Here's the rub: many of them are normal people. *Normal people.* Not Mozart. Their fame came because they 1) came up with an idea that no one else had, and 2) acted on it.

---

1 With apologies to Anakin Skywalker and Chancellor Palpatine.

2 With apologies to Mr. Beast for, well, really just not knowing much about him.

This very closely matches an academic definition of creativity: *the ability to generate ideas that are novel and useful.* "Novel" here means "new, unheard of, or never before seen in this specific way," and "useful" means that people get some use out of it, like enjoyment or a tool.

That ability requires a very specific set of skills, including *Divergent Thinking, Convergent Thinking,* and *Planning.* The people who can create a novel idea, make a use for it, and become famous for it, can do those things very well.

Before I lose you, let me get to the next point very quickly.

<u>This is an ability that can be - and often is - learned</u>

Divergent Thinking, Convergent Thinking, and Planning.

I didn't say *magic*. I didn't say *talent*. I didn't say *gift*.

Divergent Thinking: The ability to generate many ideas.

Convergent Thinking: The ability to determine which of the many ideas are worth looking into further.

Planning: Taking the best of the ideas and deciding what to do with them.

None of these three skills require an innate gift. None of these three skills require you to be born with the ability to do them. In fact, many of the people you consider to be the most naturally creative are really good at divergent thinking, but struggle with convergent thinking and planning. Anyone suffering from "writer's block" is trying to do diverging and converging at the same time, which a well-practiced creative genius would never do.

The best athletes - Lebron James, Caitlin Clark, Serena Williams, Simone Biles, Lewis Hamilton - they practice 90% of the time and perform 10% of the time.

Too many people never *practice* being creative, then struggle to be creative when asked to, then declare themselves to be "not creative," or, even worse, "dumb."

If you *practice,* you will be in command of your creativity. You can perform when you need to. You may even be seen as a "genius." We know this, because we know how your brain works when you practice the skills involved in creative thinking.

What you see here is an actual Google Earth photo of my childhood neighbor's house and their neighbor's house. Let me tell you the story of the faint path you can see pointed to by the arrows. It's a great example of how your brain cells work.

These two neighbors were about the same age, but a tall grass field separated their houses. Their parents didn't want them walking on the busy street, so they cut through the field. At first, it was hard, because the grass was tall and thick. But, after a while, a clearly-defined path began to form, making it easier. Finally, after a while, their dads saw that they were using this path all the time, so they got out their lawnmowers and mowed it. It created a clearly-defined almost-permanent path that could even be seen from Google Earth.

That is how your brain works when you practice a new skill: your brain cells struggle to make a path they haven't used before, but with repetition, that path becomes more and more well-defined, until eventually it becomes permanent. Learning to be creative is the same process as learning to play an instrument or learning to play a sport: practice and drill the fundamentals, and you'll become a master.

Dare I say, a "Genius."

Why listen to me?

Other than "the guy who wrote this book," who am I?

I've always been the "creative guy," even though "creative" was the euphemism my elementary school teachers used when they didn't want to say "odd" to my parents' face. I was the guy who spun elaborate stories, used tools in ways they weren't meant to be used, and could come up with a million ideas a minute. But that didn't mean I was in command of my creativity.

When I became a teacher, I noticed something interesting happening: any time I assigned a project and then showed an example, 90% of the projects wound up being just a copy of the example. I knew something had to be happening (besides "they're just lazy," which is what some other teachers tried to tell me), and I set out to discover why.[3]

That led to my thesis project for my first master's degree which required an extensive study on what is happening *in the brain* when people try to be creative, and how to turn those into habits. Turns out, creativity studies is a huge field! I read books like The Neuroscience of Creativity, journals like The Journal of Creative Behavior. Then, there's the holy grail, Applied Imagination by Alex Osborn, which launched the field of creativity studies.

I took that learning and published a teaching method called Delayed Guidance (Iowa State University, 2019), launched a consulting business that allowed me to teach businesses, teachers, and students the tools and habits needed to be creative, used it in my teaching (where today, I am a K-5 Gifted and Talented teacher), and spoke at conferences about how important it is to learn to be creative.

Speaking of how important it is to learn to be creative...

---

3 I'll explain more in a later chapter, but this is something called a "Knowledge Constraint," which is when your existing knowledge on a topic prevents you from being able to see it any other way. So, by showing an example, I was preventing them from thinking of any other way to do it.

Why is this important?

Take a moment and think of a genius.

Who came to mind? Mozart? Einstein? Picasso? What about Robin Williams? Or J.K. Rowling?

What about you?

If you didn't name yourself, why not? Is it because you look at people like Picasso or Robin Williams or J.K. Rowling and assume that, because you can't do what they can do, you're not a genius?

Never mind that Picasso and Williams and Rowling spent tens of thousands of hours perfecting their art. They were exceptionally good at their art form, but they also learned their genius.

As we've seen, with a few exceptions, geniuses are made, not born. A few people – two or three – every hundred years or so are born geniuses. People like Mozart, and Stephen Hawking, and Albert Einstein – they were born geniuses. Somehow, they wound up being born with something the rest of us don't have.

The rest of us? We all have the same thing. Two or three people every hundred years isn't enough to invent airplanes, create vaccines, electrify the world, revolutionize home computing, and fly to the moon. Those achievements belong to regular people who learned to be geniuses.

Two or three people every hundred years won't be enough to solve climate change, end racial disparity, eliminate poverty, close the achievement gap, solve world hunger, or finally build a flying car! Those achievements will go to regular people who learned to be geniuses.

There is such a thing as accidental genius, people who have flashes of brilliance and are able to do something with it. Accidental genius, and the people who use it to change the world, should be celebrated.

However, your ability to be a genius doesn't have to be accidental. Genius is the ability to combine two or more things or ideas into a new thing or idea. The ability to do this is something that can be improved with practice. With practice, we can all be a genius, and we don't have to rely on natural-born geniuses to change the world!

We need people to learn to be creative.

We need you to learn to be creative.

We need <u>you</u>.

The world depends on it.

Your mission, should you choose to accept

This book has three parts:

1. **The Creative Brain.** You will learn exactly what creativity is, what is happening in the brain when you are being creative, and how it's not magic or something you're born with.

2. **Thirty Days to Genius.** One short homework assignment every day to exercise your brain. Think of me as your coach, and this thirty days as the "90% practice" part of your experience.

3. **The Creative Problem-Solving Process**. Your playbook for game day, when you have a problem that needs a unique and creative solution. This is a repeatable process, studied for decades by psychologists, that helps people diverge, converge, and plan.

Read part 1. Follow the drills in part 2 for 30 days. Pull out part 3 when you have a problem you need to solve.

I always thought I was a creative person. Really, I was just a good divergent thinker. It wasn't until I learned these techniques that I became in command of my creativity.

You are who you are. You may not have the best brain, but you certainly don't have the worst. You just have the one you're stuck with. Practice with me, and you can become who the "caring adult" who handed you this book wanted to be: a genius.

Or, at least, you can pretend to be in a very convincing way.

Let's get started, future geniuses.

About the Author

David Dubczak is an educator, author, playwright, and occasional actor. His writing interests include history and comedy. Originally from Holmen, Wisconsin, he lives in Iowa with his wife Laura and dog Avila, whom they affectionately refer to as "Noodle."

David's plays have won awards with the World Film Festival in Cannes, the Iowa Motion Picture Association, and have advanced into the finalist rounds of national competitions such as the Screencraft Stage Play Competition.

You can read his plays and check out his other writings, with more to come, at DavidDWriter.com.

Look for "David Dubczak – Writer" on social media.

Like this book? Amazon and GoodReads reviews are essential to helping independent authors grow their brand. Please share how much you enjoyed this book!

Plays by David Dubczak

Available at www.DavidDWriter.com

Not a Murder Mystery

Charming con artist Curley stows away aboard the Mississippi Belle. When a passenger is discovered murdered, a rich socialite offers a million-dollar reward to solve the crime before reaching port. Curley hatches a plan: she disguises herself as a southern gentleman named "Abel Underwood," in order to frame him for the murder and claim the reward for herself!

But her plans run afoul of Professor Julius Mayberry (Egyptologist), who is running a scheme of his own. Famed detective Eloise Stout thinks something's amiss, and this whole thing may not be a murder mystery at all.

Real Fakes: The True Story of the Fake Spy who Saved D-Day

Juan Pujol Garcia is a Spanish chicken farmer and failed hotel manager who wants to be a British Spy in World War II. When the British reject him out of fear he's just a crazy buffoon, he does the unbelievable: encouraged by his equally eccentric wife Araceli, he tells the Germans he's a British spy and offers to be a double-agent. They believe him, and put him to work.

Eventually, the British catch on and start to use him. Using nothing but his wits, imagination, and a network of entirely made-up informants, "Agent Garbo" dupes the enemy, becomes the most important spy in World War II, and saves the invasion of Normandy from certain failure.

Quarterfinalist, Screencraft Stage Play Competition 2023

Delusions of Power

In an Oval Office meeting before President Melinda Lafayette's surgery, she scolds her son for trying to sneak around custom-made hallucinogenic drugs in a Tylenol bottle. She confiscates the bottle, throws it in her desk drawer, and then invites in Vice President Oswald Decatur, who mistakes it for the real thing and tries to cure his headache!

The president's staff tries to cover for a hallucinating and delirious vice president while trying to wrangle senators to pass a very important law and keep up with what could be an impending nuclear crisis in Turkey – which the VP keeps confusing for his dinner.

Award of Achievement – Iowa Motion Picture Awards, 2020
Finalist – Screencraft Stage Play Competition, 2019

Steeple

Pastor Ted arrives for his first assignment: try to save the nearly-dead Bright Hills Community Church. The dozen quirky and inept members who are left are just fine with the way things are. Pastor Ted's big dreams cause comic conflict the elderly council president, nearly-deaf organist, his ex-girlfriend, atheist secretary... and his big-time lawyer mother keeps interfering as well.

Pastor Ted has one year to save it, or the church closes forever. Perhaps it's beyond saving.

Digging Deeper (a One-Act comedy)

Billionaire Blake Anders must find two people to vouch he's a good person in order to go "upstairs" when he dies. Hilarity ensues when this proves harder than he thought.

<u>Books by David Dubczak</u>
www.DavidDWriter.com

Fiction - For Adults

Decalogue Deception
Honorable Mention, Writer's Digest
Self-Published Book Awards, 2025

Screenplay – For Adults

Guiltless
Winner – Best Original Script
World Film Festival in Cannes, 2025

Fiction – For Young Adults

Jasper Berry and the Order of the Time Watchers

Self-Help, for Teens and Tweens

How to Write a Play
Activate your Genius Mode

Historical Fiction, for Young Readers
DASH: The Carpathia's Mad Race to Rescue Titanic
Torpedoed! Surviving the Lusitania

www.ingramcontent.com/pod-product-compliance
Lightning Source LLC
Chambersburg PA
CBHW050537160726

48003CB00002B/641